EHR Governance

Organizations spend large amounts of money to purchase, deploy, and optimize their Electronic Health Records (EHRs). They are not plug-n-play systems so a commitment to an ongoing improvement cycle is necessary. When done well, this responds to the people, the process, and the technology. When not done well, complete failure of the system could result in costing the organization thousands of dollars.

Based on the foundational premise that EHR governance done right speeds up change and leads to a positive user experience, this book draws upon more than a decade of work with government, academic, and non-profit organizations using Epic, Allscripts, McKesson, Meditech, and Cerner. Designed to be practical and pragmatic, it outlines a strategic process that can scale to small and large organizations alike. It begins with how to articulate a clear vision to organizational leaders so they can champion strong EHR governance both theoretically and financially. It then walks through each step required for leading successful change, calling out critical lessons learned to help the reader avoid pitfalls and achieve measurable improvement more rapidly. It concludes with a commitment to ongoing growth and refinement through benchmarked metrics, innovation, and out-of-the-box thinking.

EHR Governance

A Practical Guide to User Centric, Consensus Driven Optimization

Paula Scariati

HIMSS

Routledge
Taylor & Francis Group

A PRODUCTIVITY PRESS BOOK

Routledge/a Productivity Press Book

First published 2023
by Routledge
605 Third Avenue, New York, NY 10158

and by Routledge
2 Park Square, Milton Park, Abingdon, Oxon, OX14 4RN

Routledge is an imprint of the Taylor & Francis Group, an informa business

© 2023 Paula Scariati

ISBN: 978-0-367-44225-5 (hbk)
ISBN: 978-0-367-40392-8 (pbk)
ISBN: 978-1-003-00840-8 (ebk)

DOI: 10.4324/9781003008408

Typeset in Garamond
by Deanta Global Publishing Services, Chennai, India

In Service, With Love

Contents

Preface..xi

Acknowledgements...xiii

About the Author..xv

SECTION 1 CONTEXT

1 **Why Governance**..**3**

    EHRs Are Not Plug-n-Play Systems 3

    Make It Easy to Do the Right Thing 8

    Burnout and Moral Injury...12

    Chapter Summary 16

    Chapter Exercises..17

2 **When Governance**...**19**

    Earlier Is Better 19

    Setting Expectations and Priorities..21

    Voice of the Customer 27

    Chapter Summary 31

    Chapter Exercises..32

3 **How Governance**...**33**

    Governance Dependencies...33

    Software Needs for EHR Governance 41

    A Roadmap for Leading Change..43

    Chapter Summary 48

    Chapter Exercises..49

SECTION 2 CHANGE

4 Create Urgency..**53**
   The Eisenhower Box..53
   Solution Jumping..56
   The Case for a Good Business Case 58
   Chapter Summary 64
   Chapter Exercises 65

5 Form a Powerful Coalition...**67**
   It's a Team Sport 67
   We're in This Together..71
   Try To See It My Way 75
   Chapter Summary 78
   Chapter Exercises 79

6 Create a Vision and a Strategy..**81**
   Core Values 81
   Governance Framework 84
   Decision-Making Bodies...90
   Design Standards..94
   Chapter Summary 101
   Chapter Exercises 102

7 Communicate the Vision **103**
   Assumptions Are the Termites of Communication...............103
   Communication Skills and Traditions..................................105
   Who Told You That? 109
   Chapter Summary 113
   Chapter Exercises 114

8 Remove Obstacles **115**
   The Allure of Inertia 115
   Change is the Only Constant in Life...................................117
   Resistance is Futile..120
   Confusion over Decision Rights 123
   Chapter Summary 125
   Chapter Exercises 126

9 Generate Short-Term Wins..**127**
   One Size Doesn't Fit All..127
   The Pain of Documentation 130
   Tell a Story with the Data...133

    Chapter Summary 137
    Chapter Exercises 138

10 Consolidate Gains and Produce More Wins 139
    Automate 139
    Scale 140
    Virtual Governance 146
    Chapter Summary 151
    Chapter Exercises 152

11 Anchor New Approaches in the Culture 153
    Culture Eats Strategy for Breakfast 153
    Culture Styles 156
    The Way We Do Things around Here 159
    Chapter Summary 164
    Chapter Exercises 165

SECTION 3 COMMITMENT

12 User Experience 169
    People, Process, and Technology 169
    The KLAS Arch Collaborative 172
    Onboarding New Physicians 178
    Chapter Summary 182
    Chapter Exercises 183

13 Accelerating Change through Innovation 185
    Intrapreneurship and Entrepreneurship 185
    Design Thinking 188
    Never Waste a Good Crisis 192
    Chapter Summary 195
    Chapter Exercises 196

14 It's a Journey Not a Destination 197
    Order Set Management 197
    Legal and Ethical Considerations 203
    Land and Expand 206
    Chapter Summary 214
    Chapter Exercises 215

Epilogue 217

Notes 219

Index 225

Preface

EHR Governance – A Practical Guide to User Centric, Consensus Driven Optimization is a roadmap for developing or optimizing the processes used to govern your electronic health record. This model, designed to be sponsored by the highest level of leadership and driven by the voice of the customer, is physician-led, consensus-driven, end-user responsive, and vendor-agnostic. If you are inclined toward a more autocratic, top-down governance model, this book is not for you.

The notion that this information could be a valuable tool for sister organizations and colleagues occurred following a 2018 HIMSS presentation. I took the stage in a conference hall at the Venetian-Palazzo-Sands Expo Center in Las Vegas and watched with surprise as over 500 people crowded into the room to hear me present *Optimizing EHR Governance to Improve the User Experience.* My moderator, noting the expression on my face chuckled, *don't look so shocked, this is a hot topic.* I spent the next hour sharing the governance journey of a large healthcare system, showing data and offering tips. While the information shared was both innovative and successful, the response that followed was unexpected. An engaging question-and-answer session was followed by a long line of audience members with requests for further consultation resulting in months of email exchanges, telephone conversations, and a few additional meetings. The appetite for guidance on EHR governance was strong, with the available information being limited and inconsistent.

Shortly thereafter, a vendor approached me about writing a chapter on EHR governance in a book they were compiling. I approached my boss regarding the opportunity, who responded *our team should write that book.* To my delight a handful of team members agreed and we drafted a proposal that was immediately accepted by this book's publisher. Over the next few months, we developed the book's framework and began writing. Unfortunately, that original group was pulled in different directions while the company reorganized as part of a merger. Within a year I was working for a new organization, navigating a large EHR go live, while an evolving COVID pandemic challenged the capabilities of many EHRs to respond to rapid change in a nimble fashion. The call for crisp, agile EHR governance was greater than ever.

Today, many health systems find themselves with bloated information technology portfolios that include multiple EHRs or several disparate instances of a single EHR. Even the rare organization with a single, mature, well-optimized EHR has usually unintentionally burdened providers with voluminous, often meaningless, documentation contributing to job dissatisfaction and burn out. In response, HIMSS has prioritized an initiative to reduce the EHR documentation burden to 25% of its current level by 2025. This *25 by 5 Symposium* suggested this goal could be achieved by focusing on six domains: (1) reimbursement, (2) regulation, (3) quality, (4) usability, (5) interoperability, and (6) self-imposed functionality. While long overdue, this initiative is dependent upon robust EHR governance to determine what gets included and (more importantly) what gets removed from an organization's EHR.

Living and breathing EHR governance day-to-day and capturing those processes in a succinct and useful manner for others to use are two different things. It was tempting to share every tip, trick, win, and lesson learned in hope that you, the reader, would travel a smoother road to a successful EHR governance process in a fraction of the time. However, knowing that each organization's EHR governance journey will (and should) look different based upon the starting point, available resources, and overarching objectives, I refrained.

For ease of navigation, this book is organized into three sections: (1) context, (2) change, and (3) commitment. Context provides the value proposition in support of the EHR governance model proposed. Change is a step-by-step breakdown of processes with suggestions and examples. Commitment is a deeper dive into areas that will anchor your work, assist your expansion, and promote innovation. If time is of the essence, focus on the summary at the end of each chapter and complete the suggested exercises. This will deliver high-level concepts and engage you in creating the framework for an EHR Governance Toolkit, a key resource and education document.

I hope this book becomes a useful tool and cherished resource. If you can, please email and share your organization's experience with EHR governance. I'd love to hear from you.

Paula Scariati

Acknowledgements

This book reflects the hard work of several amazing teams that I have had the good fortune to work with. Bill Hersh and his informatics staff at OHSU infected me with a love for informatics and an ongoing commitment to being driven by the data. Joe Colorafi hired me directly out of fellowship training and threw me into the real world of EHR go lives and governance. Members of his team, specifically Deb Stottlemyer and Maninder Khalsa, were generous mentors and friends. Mark Zielazinski instilled the value of daily rounding to connect with end users and identify issues proactively when they are small and manageable. Shez Partovi taught me to be agile, transparent, and equitable. Michael Chilton amazed me with his unique talent for mapping almost any process into a one-page workflow diagram. Katie Peterson, David Green, and Melissa McFarland inspired me with their articulate, meticulous, charismatic natures, and their inexhaustible ability to run toward every challenge with a can-do mindset. Colin Irving and Glenda Colahan orchestrated many physician governance team meetings with great care and finesse. They made it look easy, but it wasn't. Cassandra Baquir fed my love for data as we developed dashboards, OKRs, KPIs, and more. Kayla Nunez packed a powerful punch with her ardent problem-solving skills. Michael Marino touched me with his integrity. Brett Daniel generously shared lessons learned knowing that was the path to process improvement. And Tiffany Strango was my trusted partner and emotional intelligence in action.

Beyond the walls of the institutions where I've worked, several key people deserve sincere appreciation. Andrew Wilding, my provider success manager at KLAS, graciously partnered in benchmarking data from the Arch Collaborative. Conner Bice, Director of Operations for the Arch Collaborative, aided with identifying the organizational use cases woven into the book. Brittany Witt, Managing Director & Senior Advisor at the

TrustWorks Collective, kindly reviewed this book from a layperson perspective offering critical comments on content, flow, readability, and consistency. Kristine Rynne Mednansky, my editor at Taylor & Francis Group, provided patient and thoughtful encouragement as I traversed a merger, a job change, a cross-country move, and the COVID-19 pandemic. There's a reason that she's done what she does for 30 years.

Finally, my husband, Dr. Giovanni Elia. I was once told that if you love deeply and are loved deeply by just one other person in your lifetime, you've lived a good life. By that standard, I've lived a very good life. I've known Giovanni for over 35 years as a friend, partner, and colleague. His keen mind, compassion, and wit challenge and enchant me every day. His ongoing support of this book, and his thoughtful review of the final document have made it all the better.

I have been blessed with dynamic, innovative mentors, exceptional colleagues, and generous friends who have all added greatly to the content and quality of this book. Any errors or omissions are entirely my own.

About the Author

Paula Scariati, DO, MPH, MS, is a Preventive Medicine & Public Health physician specialty trained in informatics, who loves using technology to improve patient access and care. With more than 25 years of experience in government, academic, private, and nonprofit organizations, Paula's approach to digital transformation combines her unique clinical perspective with her expertise in medical informatics, governance, and change management. Throughout her career, she's partnered with high-performing, multi-functional teams in fast-paced environments to develop innovative apps, lead EHR go lives, optimize workflows, and map improvement processes. Her work is data driven, and at the heart of everything she does is an unrelenting commitment to user experience. Paula's informatics repertoire spans the continuum of care using software tools from Allscripts, McKesson, Meditech, Cerner, and Epic, along with ADT, CDI, population health, and best of breed platforms.

A seasoned national speaker, an award-winning medical school instructor, and an ASQ Lean Six Sigma Green Belt, Paula has authored over 100 articles including 14 peer review publications. In her free time, she enjoys tackling house remodeling projects and refining her Italian language skills. She can be reached for a curbside consult or a more formal engagement through LinkedIn or by email at Paula.Scariati@fastmail.com.

CONTEXT

1

Without context, a piece of information is just a dot. It floats in your brain with a lot of other dots and doesn't mean a damn thing.

Knowledge is information-in-context ... connecting the dots.

– Michael Ventura

DOI: 10.4324/9781003008408-1

Chapter 1

Why Governance

If you think good design is expensive, you should look at the cost of bad design.

– Dr. Ralf Speth, CEO, Jaguar Land Rover

EHRs Are Not Plug-n-Play Systems

In more than a dozen years as an informatician in organizations ranging from community hospitals to large enterprise healthcare systems, there was never a question that the Electronic Health Record (EHR) required an ongoing improvement cycle. It was evident that the EHR was disruptive to all except the most tech savvy of providers and that governance was the key to reigning in the chaos and unintended consequences associated with the emerging digital world of healthcare. Documentation needs increased, provider–patient face time decreased, workflows were discombobulated, and regulatory requirements mounted. Today, with the clarity of retrospective vision, it seems absurd that a piece of software would ever require such a detailed level of attention driven by the organization or end users using it. Imagine if you needed to govern your Microsoft Office Suite or Adobe software. The design of your smartphone is elegant and intuitive as are the apps you choose to launch on it. Design thinking is the life blood of software engineers devoted to creating a pleasurable user experience. So why wasn't this the case with the EHR?

DOI: 10.4324/9781003008408-2

EHR 1.0, the initial version of EHR software, was formally birthed after a somewhat protracted gestation, on Tuesday, February 17, 2009, when the Health Information Technology for Economic and Clinical Health (HITECH) Act was signed into law. The idea of making America's health records electronic wasn't new and had been fashionable in Washington DC for many years. George W. Bush laid a foundation for this during his presidency by creating the Office of the National Coordinator (ONC). But funding was never secured during his presidency for broad implementation. Then President Barack Obama, four weeks after his election, pitched his plan in a radio address.

> We will make sure that every doctor's office and hospital in this country is using cutting edge technology and electronic medical records so that we can cut red tape, prevent medical mistakes and help save billions of dollars each year.[1]

Praised as a win for all, this proposal was readily embraced as a long-needed uplift to the American healthcare system with the upside of infusing $31 billion into an economy struggling to recover from the severe economic downturn later labeled the great recession. At the time it was enacted, HITECH was considered by many to be the most important piece of healthcare legislation to be passed in the last 20–30 years.

While this was unfolding, I was making a transition in my medical career. I had recently moved to San Diego and was looking for a complement to my patient care responsibilities. As I actively searched, a colleague asked if I was interested in an online education opportunity designed to learn more about medical informatics. Having no idea what medical informatics was, I inquired. The American Medical Informatics Association (AMIA) defined informatics as an emerging physician subspecialty focused on using data, information, and knowledge to improve human health and the delivery of healthcare services.[2] Intrigued, I enrolled in the virtual program offered by Oregon Health Sciences University (OHSU) in Portland, Oregon. A little over a month into the training I knew I was in love with what I was learning, so I contacted my instructor, Dr. Bill Hersh, and asked how I could formally train in medical informatics. His program at OHSU was recruiting to fill several National Library of Medicine (NLM) Fellowship positions, so I applied and was accepted. Two months later I was attending my first classes in Portland as an NLM Informatics Fellow. I immersed myself in my newfound passion with classes in organizational behavior, JAVA programming, software engineering, and more. It was now September 2009 and I watched from my training cocoon as the details of the HITECH Act unfolded.

The goal of this massive stimulus was not just to get healthcare organizations and physicians to buy EHRs, but rather to get them using EHRs in a way that would improve safety, quality, and patient experience. To do this, a carrot-and-stick approach was devised where physicians could qualify for up to $64,000 in incentives (over a period of years) if they jumped through a series of hoops meant to demonstrate that they were meaningful users of their EHR technology. This was a bold undertaking since the proposed ideal – a useful, interoperable, nationwide records system – was *utterly infeasible to get to in a short time frame*, said Farzad Mostashari, who joined the ONC as deputy director in 2009 and became its leader in 2011. That didn't stop the federal planners from pursuing their grand ambitions. The stakeholders convened for input had big ideas for EHRs. The Food and Drug Administration (FDA) wanted to track unique device identifiers for medical implants, the Centers for Disease Control and Prevention (CDC) wanted to support epidemiology and emergent outbreak monitoring, the Centers for Medicare & Medicaid Services (CMS) wanted to capture a series of quality metrics, and so on. *We had all the right ideas that were discussed and hashed out by the committee*, said Mostashari, *but they were all of the right ideas.*[3]

Vendors, focused on getting their software certified and deployed, weren't given adequate time and didn't have the resources required to hone usability or workflow design. This work, while recognized as important, wasn't key to getting a minimum viable product out the door. In fact, vendors had their hands full for some time keeping pace with the features and functionalities required to meet the meaningful use metrics stipulated to qualify for the federal incentive dollars available. Few controls were imposed, so doctors could shop for bargain-price software packages at Costco and Walmart's Sam's Club – where eClinicalWorks sold a turnkey system for $11,925 – and cash in on the government's adoption incentives.

It took years for user experience design work to become a higher priority for EHR vendors. Even then, under mounting pressure to introduce new features faster, many vendors took an inside-out approach, wherein new functionality was developed by internal experts and engineers in a vacuum. The importance of market and end-user insight remained poorly appreciated. Meanwhile poor user interface design was being reported in the medical literature as impacting care delivery and workflows. A growing chorus of providers was complaining about longer work weeks, low-value documentation tasks, less face time with patients, and difficult-to-navigate systems. The EHR and those associated with it were quickly becoming the enemy.

One large enterprise organization tackled this problem head-on by developing a provider-centric vision for an EHR 2.0 paradigm empowered with resources and leadership. This shift engaged providers as partners and used a three-prong approach to improve EHR usability: (1) training informaticians, (2) EHR governance, and (3) data-driven optimization.

Training informaticians was a workforce development initiative focused on developing an informatics support team with a standardized set of skills. This provided the strong foundation required for the other parts of the program since strong, boots-on-the-ground, at-the-elbow support was seen as the cornerstone of success. This investment in people was intended, over time, to grow an expert cohort of informaticians that could be given control over EHR build with localized impact.

EHR governance was redesigned to be provider centric and consensus driven. Providers were empowered to work with their informatics team resources to translate the problems they were experiencing into change request tickets. Each request then passed through a gatekeeper committee tasked with ensuring a sound business case and technical feasibility. Next, physician-impacting changes were reviewed and voted upon by a group comprised of specialty-appropriate physician representatives from each region in the organization. A majority vote of a group quorum moved a request forward. An app, which worked much like the tracking system used by UPS, was developed to allow easy monitoring of all change requests through their governance lifecycle.

Requiring data to drive optimization was key to shifting the EHR culture toward evidence-driven workflows and platform optimization. Initially this work began with localized site visits that, informed by time, motion, and use metrics, focused on rapid cycle improvement. As the quality of data available matured, so too did the process. Informaticians were trained in tools and techniques which allowed for a broader application of the process. Further enhancements in and automation of the data led to improved scalability with more targeted and proactive engagement.

With time, a consistent unwavering devotion to the user's experience – driven by workforce education, EHR governance, and data-informed optimization – grew a culture of trust between providers and the informatics team. There were still many problems to be solved, but processes were perceived as fair, equitable, transparent, and accountable. Decision-body voice and choice, the very heart of EHR governance values, returned some level of mastery, autonomy, and purpose to physicians.

The next step on this journey was a tipping point marked by a shift from change requests that were transactional in nature to change requests that were transformative (Figure 1.1). This transition to an EHR 3.0 paradigm occurred organically for many organizations as the maturity of both the provider and the EHR build evolved. Change requests became more complex with a greater focus on evidence-based medicine (EBM), policy, and clinical outcomes. Concerns of system integration, interoperability, and decision support reflected an understanding that the EHR system was mission-critical to healthcare delivery and must be integrated into a myriad of other information systems to provide a seamless patient experience.

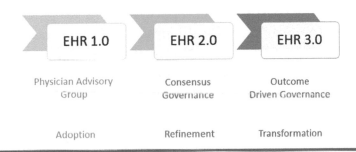

Figure 1.1   A representation of the evolution of EHR governance processes. It began with the initial adoption of the software (EHR 1.0), and then transitioned toward refinement and optimization (EHR 2.0), finally maturing into an agent of transformation driving outcomes (EHR 3.0).

In his book *The Digital Doctor*,[4] Dr. Robert Wachter, Professor and Chair of Medicine at the University of California, San Francisco, arrives at a similar destination by passing through what he describes as the four stages of Health Information Technology (HIT):

1. Digitize the record.
2. Connect the parts.
3. Draw meaningful insight from the data.
4. Translate the insights into action that improves value.

If EHR 1.0 and 2.0 were focused on digitizing the medical record, EHR 3.0 (10 years and $40 billion after HITECH was signed into law) was now engaged with making headway on items 2, 3, and 4.

The last few years have seen a renewed focus on connecting the parts with legislation now endorsing national standards and CMS leading the charge to promote information sharing and interoperability. As healthcare systems and entrepreneurs respond with new and exciting innovation, the scope of EHR governance will grow. Instead of simply brokering change requests, EHR governance will need to remain nimble and responsive to technological advances – to demonstrate outcomes such as reduced variability and waste together with improved clinical care and customer satisfaction.

Make It Easy to Do the Right Thing

It is impossible for physicians to keep pace with the knowledge explosion in medicine[5]. The number of medical journals has more than quadrupled since 1970 translating into roughly 6,000 articles per day or one new article every 30 seconds. Care complexity has similarly mushroomed.[6] A private practitioner may interact with 200 or more other physicians in over 100 practices to meet the needs of their Medicare population. Intensive care physicians engage in 180 activities per patient each day, and chronic disease patients often suffer with multiple comorbid conditions requiring the management of long lists of medications. The translation of science into evidence and then into care at the bedside is slow resulting in missed opportunities, waste, harm, and a suboptimal patient experience. While the solution to these problems requires a coordinated, cross-disciplinary effort, technology can assist.

Technology can be leveraged to continuously and reliably capture, curate, and deliver the best evidence available to guide, support, tailor, and improve clinical decision-making, care safety, and quality. With time, this will automate the work done by services like UpToDate® which employs over 6,300 physicians to distill the medical literature into useful synopses for practicing doctors. Tools like natural language processing, machine learning, and other forms of artificial intelligence (AI) will allow us to offer best practice information in the context of real-time, patient-specific data. The result will be tailored suggestions to practitioners regarding the application of knowledge for care improvement unique to their specific patient. This augmented decision support of the future will be the natural evolution of the clinical decision support (CDS) of today (Figure 1.2).

02

Understanding CDS

CDS is **not** simply an alert, notification, or explicit care suggestion. CDS encompasses a variety of tools including, but not limited to:

- Computerized alerts and reminders for providers and patients
- Clinical guidelines
- Condition-specific order sets
- Focused patient data reports and summaries
- Documentation templates
- Diagnostic support
- Contextually relevant reference information

These functionalities may be deployed on a variety of platforms (e.g. mobile, cloud-based, installed).[2] CDS is not intended to replace clinician judgment, but rather to provide a tool to assist care team members in making timely, informed, and higher quality decisions.

The "CDS Five Rights" concept[3] provides a best practice framework that may be helpful when considering CDS options appropriate for a practice. The CDS Five Rights concept states that in order to provide benefits, CDS interventions must provide:

- the right information (evidence-based guidance, response to clinical need)

Figure 1.2 Guidance from the Centers for Medicare & Medicaid Services on the scope and the utility of clinical decision support within the EHR. Source: The Centers for Medicare & Medicaid Services.

To utilize CDS to integrate best practice clinical knowledge into care decisions, one must strike the right balance between providing practitioners with useful, actionable evidence and disrupting their patient care engagement with low-value information. This sounds simpler than it is since what one practitioner sees as a welcome reminder, another may see as a nuisance break in workflow. And some CDS, useful early on for educating to a new best practice or standard, may over time wane in value.

Until practitioners can customize how CDS works to meet their individual needs, EHR governance is the key to designing and deploying provider-friendly CDS logic. To do this, governance leverages validated design theory like the five rights:

- The right information,
- To the right person,
- In the right format,
- Through the right channel,
- At the right time in the workflow.

Right Information

To the extent possible, the information presented in the EHR should be data driven. This means it should be evidence-based, adopted from well-respected guidelines, or based on national performance measures. In the case of a 41-year-old female thought to be at average risk for developing breast cancer, an alert is generated informing the physician that a shared decision-making conversation with the patient is required to determine whether a screening mammogram is appropriate. The alert is based upon 2009 guidelines from the United States Preventive Services Task Force that indicate a lack of evidence to support universal mammography screening for women in their 40s at average risk for developing breast cancer.

The CDS offered, in this case an alert, should cause as little disruption as possible, be understandable, and be actionable. At one end of the disruption spectrum, the alert may be offered passively through a banner or zone in the EHR that doesn't interfere with the main work of the provider. At the other end of the disruption spectrum, the alert may be deployed through a pop-up that blocks any additional work from being done until it is addressed. The information contained within the alert must strike a proper balance. Too much information may induce a cognitive overload causing the provider to ignore or override the message. Too little information, forcing the provider to access other parts of the chart for additional information, may also result in the provider bypassing the message and complaining of alert fatigue. Finally, the alert should be actionable. If the provider may need to order a test in response to the alert, it should be easy to do that. In the current example, the physician has a conversation with the patient and learns of a risk factor, not currently documented within the EHR, that makes screening mammography appropriate. The alert makes documenting that risk factor easy and allows the provider to order the test with a single click.

Right Person

Care teams are here to stay so it is important that the right information gets to the right person who can then act. In addition to a provider, that right person might be a medical assistant, a physical therapist, a pharmacist, a chaplain, or perhaps a case worker. In the example above, the physician received and actioned the initial alert. But what if the patient never went for the screening mammogram? Some type of follow-up reminder or report might go to the medical assistant for additional follow-up. The key is to present information only to the individual(s) who can act.

Right Format

There are different ways of getting information into the hands of the right people. The example above entailed an alert, but CDS can be delivered within order sets, protocols, patient monitoring systems, info buttons, apps, and more. The secret to choosing the best format for delivering information is to clearly define the problem being solved. It is useful to have an inventory of current systems to determine which CDS tools are readily available, which tools need to be developed in-house, and which tools need to be purchased through a vendor.

Right Channel

Well-designed CDS within the EHR can be nuanced and delivered through a number of different channels. In the example above, the alert may have been delivered through an active pop-up that triggered a soft or hard stop in the provider's workflow. It may have also been sent passively as a message in a designated zone within the screen real estate of the EHR. CDS may also be conveyed through patient portals, computerized provider order entry, apps, reports, or paper.

Right Time in Workflow

When it comes to act in response to CDS, timing is everything. In the above example, if the physician was alerted about the screening mammogram after the patient left and she was writing her note, she wouldn't have been able to have the conversation that determined that the screening test was, in fact, appropriate for this patient. Likewise, an allergy or drug–drug interaction that triggers after a prescription has been ordered is much less useful than one that triggers in real time when the physician is searching for the medication to place the order or write the prescription. A common example of this problem occurs when a physician is treating a patient who is taking aspirin as a preventive measure. The physician temporarily loses track of this and prescribes Coumadin. After entering all the information for the prescription, the physician attempts to send the order to the pharmacy. An alert appears warning of a possible drug–drug interaction between the aspirin and the Coumadin. However, it would have been much more advantageous for the physician to be alerted when he began typing the word Coumadin at the start of the prescription writing process.

The path forward is clear. For a CDS implementation process to be successful, the clinical processes involved must be thoroughly understood and documented so that the right information is delivered to the right person at the right time – making it easy to do the right thing. Automation, through newfound technological capabilities and better connectivity, will rapidly scale these processes placing vast medical knowledge at the practitioner's fingertips. Linking this information with patient-specific data will allow AI-driven systems to provide customized recommendations to the practitioner, who can adjust their care engagement and deliver personalized medicine.

Burnout and Moral Injury

Ask a random sample of physicians about burnout and the topic of their EHR will surely come up. EHRs started out with the noble goals of improving safety, quality, interoperability, and communication. Over the last 12 years, however, they have morphed into tools for capturing core measures, meaningful use metrics, and documentation improvement, adding an ever-growing number of keystrokes and clicks to the physician's day. Physicians are frustrated that a sacred tradition of healing has been reduced to a commodity overburdened by regulation with the physician–patient relationship now defined by scores, algorithmic logic, and economies of scale. The triad of exhaustion, low productivity, and a feeling of deep cynicism defines burnout, but this term resonates poorly with many physicians who come from a tradition of honing their resourcefulness and resilience through intense training and demanding work. These sacrifices were, historically, a rite of passage rewarded by the intimacies of a calling that offered the privilege of serving and making a difference in patient's lives. Today growing piles of paperwork, longer hours, and reduced autonomy have slowly eroded the amount of time a physician has to spend with the patient, impacting the very heart of their chosen profession. Drs. Wendy Dean and Simon Talbot more accurately define this phenomenon in clinicians as moral injury, not burnout.[7]

To better understand physician moral injury, the National Academy of Medicine (NAM) developed a conceptual framework of the issue, broken into seven categories (Table 1.1).[8] Four of those categories are external factors (related to workload and the environment in which a clinician is practicing medicine) and three are internal factors (related to personal skills, abilities, and roles).

Table 1.1   **Factors Affecting Clinician Well-Being and Resilience**

External Factors	*Internal Factors*
Sociocultural	**Healthcare Role**
Culture of safety and transparency	Alignment of responsibility and authority
Social determinants of health	Administrative responsibilities
Stigmatize mental health	Patient population and clinical responsibilities
Regulatory, Business, and Payor Environment	**Personal Factors**
Accreditation and quality ratings	Sense of meaning
Documentation and reporting requirements	Work-life integration
Insurance company policies	Lack of engagement/connection to meaning and purpose in work
Organizational Factors	**Skills and Abilities**
Bureaucracy and power dynamics	Mastering new technologies or potential use of technology
Data collection requirements	Optimizing workflow
Level of support for all healthcare team members	Organization and communication skills
Learning/Practice Environment	
Health Information Technology interoperability and usability/EHR autonomy	
Collaborative versus competitive environment	

Source: Adapted from National Academy of Medicine, *Taking Action against Clinician Burnout: A Systems Approach to Professional Well-Being. https://nam.edu/systems-approaches-to-improve-patient-care-by-supporting-clinician-well-being/*

Many organizations have shifted their approach to moral injury to address its external causes, like sociocultural, regulatory, business, payer and organizational factors. This is a good beginning. Hospitals also are providing more on-site opportunities for clinicians to practice self-care, like exercise machines, time-out rooms, and gardens. However, this resilience training approach implies that the provider needs fixing. If only they could cope better, they would be okay. This has been likened to repeatedly punching someone and then giving them Motrin for the pain. Prevention is far more effective than treatment.[9]

I recently saw Dr. Nisha Mehta,[10] a well-known writer, speaker, and physician advocate, speak at an innovation conference near my home. Dr. Mehta is a musculoskeletal radiologist by training, so I found her metaphor about burnout quite compelling:

> As a musculoskeletal radiologist, I frequently think about stress fractures versus insufficiency fractures. You probably don't, so as a refresher, a stress fracture is abnormal stress on normal bone, and an insufficiency fracture is normal stress on abnormal bone. So, your stress fracture is the 21-year-old college student who decides it's a good idea to run three marathons in a month (normal bone, abnormal stress), while your insufficiency fracture is when grandma comes to visit and trips over your child's Legos, breaking multiple bones (abnormal bone, normal stress). I feel that the average physician is made of pretty strong bone. If you want to take that nerdy analogy further, our T-score on a DEXA scan would be unequivocally positive. We've survived over a decade of training that is rigorous mentally, emotionally, and physically, and therefore, I'd say that most graduates are quite resilient. So, in my mind, physician burnout is much more of a "stress fracture" than an "insufficiency fracture".

Maintaining EHRs has morphed into almost a full-time job. A 2017 study showed that, for every average 11.4-hour workday, clinicians in southern Wisconsin spent nearly 6 hours in their hospital's EHR system.[11] That means doctors were spending less of their day building relationships and treating patients, and more time entering data – often after they'd left the office.

One suggestion for alleviating the administrative burden on physicians is outsourcing or automating these duties. For example, in the emergency department (ED) setting, some studies report that medical scribes increased efficiency. Personally, I've found two camps on the matter. Camp 1 is home to the ED physicians who love scribes and use them religiously. ED physicians in camp 2 feel that scribes slow them down and require a great deal of training. This group prefers voice-to-text technology and shortcuts like macros to optimize their workflow.

Another way to reduce the burden that EHRs place on physicians, the focus of this book, is to champion physician autonomy in EHR governance. Empower doctors with voice and choice to make rational, safe, evidence-based and financially-responsible decisions about the scope of the work that they do and workflow efficiencies. Change driven by top-down authoritarian mandates on medical practice is degrading and ultimately ineffective.[12]

Chapter Summary

- The initial software development lifecycle of EHRs (EHR 1.0) was unusual and driven by federal financial incentives. Early on, EHR systems were engineered to meet meaningful use metrics with little emphasis on user experience.

- As healthcare organizations rapidly adopted various EHRs, there was a transition to post-deployment refinement and optimization (EHR 2.0). Here, the value proposition of designing a robust user interface and experience came into focus and the benefits of EHR governance became evident.

- As both organizations and software companies matured, there was an organic shift from transactional change requests to transformational ones. Here, a more refined EHR governance aligned with organizational goals, objectives, and outcomes (EHR 3.0). These EHRs, while much more user friendly, still rely upon a solid governance strategy to personalize and optimize functionality to meet end-user needs.

- Good EHR governance makes it easy for the end user to do the right thing. This includes functionality that synthesizes, digests, and translates the large amount of medical knowledge published daily.

- Clinical decision support is defined by five rights: getting the right information, to the right person, in the right format, through the right channel, at the right time in the workflow.

- Governance can also help alleviate some of the unintended consequences associated with digitizing the medical record. It returns some semblance of mastery, autonomy, and purpose to providers.

- Burnout is not a problem with provider resilience. Burnout is a problem with low-value, time-consuming tasks.

Chapter Exercises

Throughout many of the end-of-chapter exercises in this book, you'll be defining key components of an EHR Governance Toolkit that will house the details of your organization's governance processes. This will include your mission and objectives, scope, resources, roles and responsibilities, parliamentary procedure, team operations, and more. This Toolkit will be the key to process improvement, new employee training, preserving company knowledge, risk mitigation, and operational consistency. As your governance matures, this document will grow to include case studies, best practices and models that reflect real-time needs and lessons learned.

Let's begin by defining your mission – the *why* for standing up or refining an EHR governance structure. Grab a pad of paper and answer a few questions to get the juices flowing.

1. What do you want your EHR governance to do? Streamline documentation? Improve revenue capture? Reduce complaints? Improve satisfaction? Improve care efficiencies? Something else?
2. Is the process for making changes to your EHR clear to the key stakeholders?
3. Should anyone be able to request a change to the EHR or will that be limited in some way?
4. What types of EHR changes should be driven from the top-down (leaders, policy, regulations)? From the bottom-up (end users)? What percentage of requests from each group would be ideal?
5. What qualities should your governance prioritize in your EHR? Design? Safety? Quality? Experience? Something else?
6. Do you see any EHR-associated issues contributing to provider dissatisfaction and burnout? If yes, list them?

Armed with your responses to these questions, make a pass at drafting your mission statement – your *why* for EHR governance. Don't be afraid to get everything you want down on paper but then take time to wordsmith and solicit feedback to hone your why. The clarity you have now will translate downstream as we move forward.

When you've completed this exercise, you'll have the mission statement of your new EHR Governance Toolkit along with a "Chapter Exercises" working document that has the questions above with your responses.

Chapter 2

When Governance

There is never a good time for tough decisions. There will always be an election or something else. You have to pick courage and do it. Governance is about taking tough, even unpopular decisions.

– Jairam Ramesh

Earlier Is Better

The moment you decided to adopt an EHR, the need for some form of governance was inevitable. Early on this wasn't obvious and many organizations didn't have any type of EHR governance structure. In fact, in 2014, more than 5 years after the HITECH Act was signed into law, a report from HIMSS Analytics indicated that only 60% of healthcare organizations had a formalized EHR governance policy in place, and just 63% of those organizations included a multi-disciplinary advisory board or committee to monitor, suggest, and approve changes to the data governance strategy.[1] More recently, the KLAS Arch Collaborative, which has surveyed over 250 healthcare organizations around the world regarding their EHR experience, reported robust governance as a key determinant and best practice predictor of EHR satisfaction.[2]

Months before you ever deployed your EHR or had a single user log in, you were establishing the framework for what would become your EHR governance. Early adopter providers who love technology became stalwart champions of the benefits of EHR adoption and helped to rally the troops,

DOI: 10.4324/9781003008408-3

while guardian providers asked pointed and detailed questions to ensure that adopting a new digital technology didn't break more things than it improved. Key stakeholders in your organization worked with analysts and architects to make decisions about future state workflows, lab and radiology interfaces, formulary build and order sets, all of which determined what EHR 1.0 would look like. You agreed upon go-live parameters and project scope, prioritized what interfaces and functionality would be enabled for go live and what would be handled post-go live as part of refinement and optimization. You erected a command center for the first few weeks of your EHR implementation to immediately address broken functionality, build misses, and safety issues. But as soon as users engaged with the EHR in real time (and even before), requests for enhancements and optimization started to roll in. Deemed not mission-critical to a safe and successful EHR implementation, these requests were added to the parking lot list of items to be addressed post-go live. When the command center closed, that list was transitioned, and the formal work of governance began (Figure 2.1). You were now embarking upon your EHR 2.0 journey.

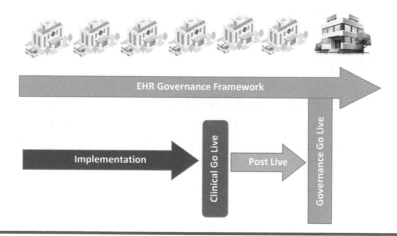

Figure 2.1   **A proposed framework for EHR governance processes is ideally laid down as part of your implementation processes. The transition to formal governance occurs several weeks post live, usually when the command center closes.**

For many organizations, EHR governance processes evolved organically in response to change requests as they were made. Perhaps you convened a steering committee or advisory group chaired by an informatics leader to vet, prioritize, and respond to the requests. In the absence of a structured, well-communicated governance process, things may have gotten confusing quickly. It was not uncommon to hear about vocal providers and administrators receiving preferential attention while front-line practitioners waited with no understanding of how, whether, or when their needs would be addressed. This may have led to practitioners in the trenches feeling marginalized and unsupported. They had just spent months learning a new system only to find that it slowed them down, burdened them with new policies and documentation, and wasn't easily changed or optimized. If these issues weren't promptly identified and solved, trust in the IT team slowly eroded and an *EHR-as-the-enemy* attitude took hold.

The bad news is that once trust is lost, regaining it is an uphill battle. It requires a well-defined, consistent process supported by crisp, clear communication. The good news is that it is never too late to begin – it can be done.

Setting Expectations and Priorities

While deploying an EHR governance structure early is better, this framework must have a mechanism for setting expectations and priorities to thwart unrealistic assumptions. Most healthcare executives and end users have little interest in the details involved in operationalizing a change request or upgrade within the EHR. They simply want results – yesterday. I secretly suspect they think of EHR changes like updating a Microsoft Word document – a few keystrokes here or there, hit save, and voila! Would that were true.

While there is little need for leaders or clinicians to grasp the nuances of these things, it is quite important that appropriate expectations be set for them around how long a change request might take with a transparent line of vision into where a change request is at any point in time. If we think about business as a metaphor for EHR governance, there are three ways of setting expectations:

1. Underpromise and overdeliver,
2. Do exactly as promised, or
3. Overpromise (and then end up under delivering).

Overpromising (item 3) is not an option in either business or EHR governance. It implies that you know what you can deliver but inflate expectations to impress others or secure the deal. When you under deliver, your credibility and reputation suffer.

Item 2 is arguably the best option but can be challenging to do consistently. Executing exactly what you've agreed to and delivering it on time is the Holy Grail of predictive analytics and expectation setting. Some organizations achieve this, in part, through service level agreements (SLAs). An SLA is a commitment to a specified turnaround time (TAT) for a defined deliverable made between an IT service provider and a customer. In the case of EHR governance, it is often a promise that a request will be completed within a certain number of days. This is difficult in the real world because you often don't have control of all the factors that impact your ability to do this; maybe someone got sick, or a supplier missed their deadline. So, if you are going to use an SLA, be prudent and build in a 25% margin just to be on the safe side. Which brings us to the first option.

Simply put, when you deliver more than what you've promised to your client and more than what they were expecting, perceived value increases. With increased value, credibility and trust grow. Sometimes you will overdeliver without even trying to do so. When this happens, just tell your end users that you always give your best and sometimes, your *best* even surprises you! Your end user will remember how well you delivered and will be much more likely to lean in your favor the next time a decision needs to be made. And when it comes to building the reputation of your EHR governance processes, there is nothing better than a bunch of satisfied customers.

A large healthcare system that I worked with declined to use SLAs for EHR change requests but rather developed a smartphone app that allowed anyone to track EHR governance change requests in real time (Figure 2.2)

Figure 2.2 **Screenshots of the uTrace™ app that was used to track the lifecycle of any EHR governance change request.**

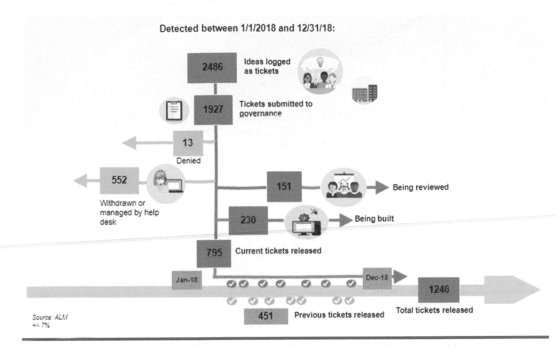

Detected between 1/1/2018 and 12/31/18:

2486 — Ideas logged as tickets

1927 — Tickets submitted to governance

13 — Denied

552 — Withdrawn or managed by help desk

151 — Being reviewed

230 — Being built

795 — Current tickets released

Jan-18 — Dec-18

1246 — Total tickets released

451 — Previous tickets released

Source: ALM
+/- 7%

Figure 2.3   Infographic of change request throughput for a large healthcare organization, calendar year 2018.

– much like UPS tracks a package. They then built interactive dashboards (Figure 2.3) to monitor throughput and TAT in real time. Dashboard thresholds automatically triggered a review of any change request that was not progressing according to certain loosely developed guidelines. This was done internally because experience had proven that TAT was variable and highly correlated with ticket complexity. Using a single, averaged SLA, regardless of ticket complexity, set unrealistic expectations for requests with a higher complexity and build burden, resulting in dissatisfaction for all. In lieu of an SLA team members engaged in conversations with end users about why something might take 90 days to operationalize while something else might take 180 days. This was more labor intensive but over time, the end users became more educated consumers of their EHR technology and would, on occasion, call out technical limitations to certain types of requests on their own.

Another approach to setting expectations, adapted from work done by our colleagues at Kaiser Permanente Northwest, is a simple yet elegant visual called the *Pyramid of Change* (Figure 2.4).[3] The pyramid provides an easy-to-understand graphic that stratifies how long one should expect a certain type of change request to take. Level 1, at the very top of the

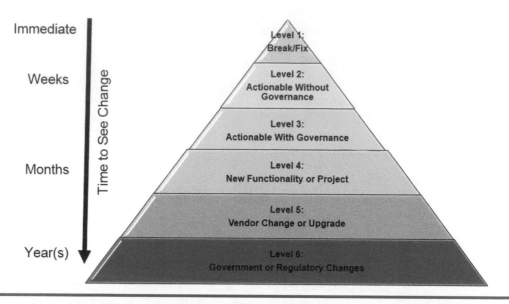

Figure 2.4   The Pyramid of Change: a tool for setting expectations around EHR governance change requests, developed by Kaiser Permanente Northwest. Source: Adapted from *https://klasresearch.com/archcollaborative/report/2019-summit-slides-individual-organization-presentations/276*.

pyramid, captures break/fix requests; it was there and working and now it's not. These requests are managed outside of normal EHR governance processes (usually by the help desk) and can be corrected rather quickly. Level 2 includes requests that won't be managed by the help desk but that don't require full blown governance processes. An example might be an *other* option missing from a dropdown menu or a build miss from a recently deployed change. Level 3 captures requests that require governance processes while level 4 includes new functionality or projects. Level 5 includes code upgrades or changes from the vendor, and level 6 is government or regulatory changes. As one moves down the levels of the pyramid, the expected time for making a change increases.

Yet another organization that I worked with opted to set expectations for EHR governance using the story of the rock, pebbles, and the sand. To summarize, the rocks are critical things (your family, your health, your children), the pebbles are other important things (your home, your car, your job), and the sand is everything else. Translated into setting expectations for EHR governance, rocks were things like safety issues and new clinical pathways, pebbles were things like medication updates and decision support, and sand was all the small optimization and broken functionality requests. The takeaway was that if you fill your jar with sand, there is no room for rocks or pebbles. However, if you fill your jar with a few rocks and some pebbles, there is still room for quite a bit of sand.

Regardless of the method you use to set expectations with your EHR governance change processes, there are a few lessons worth sharing. First, be honest when things go wrong. If you want your end users to have confidence in you, then trust them with the truth. Be open, transparent, honest, and specific. Communicate clearly and present workaround options or solutions. This reinforces that you are players on the same team working together to achieve a common goal.

Second, don't allow others to set expectations for your processes, especially if you know they are unrealistic. There are times when the impact of a change request in the EHR will be framed in terms normally reserved for describing a national pandemic, global warming, or world hunger. The urgency is beyond high and the need for immediate change is not negotiable. Occasionally a true and immediate safety concern will rise to this level of need and should be managed accordingly. However, the majority of cases where this happens are usually projects that have failed to allocate sufficient time for their processes and are now pressing frantically to make up time to meet a deadline. As soon as you become aware of these projects, preferably long before they come to you, reach out to their project manager and help them build a realistic timeline within their Gantt chart for EHR governance. This will go a long way toward preventing project delays and having governance processes viewed as obstructive.

We all live in a world of finite resources where it is neither practical nor feasible to make every EHR change requested. Change requests responding to safety issues require immediate attention and are non-negotiable (although they still require thoughtful vetting and design). Centralized requests with broad regulatory or financial impacts benefit from a well-defined scope, design, and timeline but, for the most part, are also non-negotiable. Bottom-up or end-user requests, depending on their volume and the resources available to build and deploy them, often require reconciliation, consolidation, and prioritization. This allows for similar requests from disparate sources to be merged and then ranked by importance. This can be achieved by running all end user requests through a standardized prioritization tool (Table 2.1) or convening a council tasked with this responsibility. We will discuss this in greater detail in Chapter 6.

Some measure of complexity is also recommended (Table 2.2) to discern between a request that requires 10 hours of build work and minimal

Table 2.1 Example of a Prioritization Scoring Tool That Can Be Used to Rank EHR Change Requests. A Higher Score Indicates a Higher Priority.

Prioritization Criteria	Score
Clinical severity of consequences if not implemented	0 = no consequence, 10 = potential impact, 20 = major impact
Will improve access to clinical data for patient care	No = 0, Yes = 10
Will improve access to clinical data for research	No = 0, Yes = 5
Will improve access to administrative data	No = 0, Yes = 5
Is mandated by regulatory agency	Yes = 20, No = 0
Is a mandatory upgrade (loss of support or discount if upgrade not taken)	Yes = 20, No = 0
Is there a current work around?	Yes = 0, No = 10
Does this have the potential to improve technical system performance?	Yes = 10, No = 0
Does this have the potential to streamline a workflow process?	Rank from 0 to 10: 0 = none, 10 = significant
Does this have the potential to save clinicians' time?	Rank from 0 to 10: 0 = none, 10 = significant
Quantity of users who will benefit	Rank from 0 to 20: 0 = none, 20 = all system users
Does this enhance user's experience with the system?	Rank from 0 to 10: 0 = none, 10 = significant

communication to deploy and one that requires 200 hours of build work and an intensive educational effort to deploy. This assessment is best done by someone with build expertise since it is not unusual for a seemingly innocuous request to require a time intensive build effort. This is often the case with requests requiring some form of decision logic.

Rules and alerts, for example, often require detailed algorithmic logic comprised of multiple branching nodes on a decision tree. That seemingly simple request for an alert when a patient doesn't have a current advanced directive on the chart has to cycle through a fair amount of if-then logic applied to information captured in different parts of the chart to return information that is accurate. And once that alert is triggered, it should also be smart enough to

Table 2.2   **Example of a Complexity Scoring Tool That Can be Used to Rank EHR Change Requests. A Higher Score Indicates Higher Complexity.**

Impact to Informatics Resources	Score
Work effort to complete	Rank from 0 to 10: 0 = none, 10 = significant
Availability of staff for project (right people & skill)	Available now = 0, Available within 3 months = 3, Available within 4-6 months = 6, Available within 7-12 months = 10
Project complexity rank from 0 to 10	Rank from 0 to 10: 0 = Simple, 10 = Requires extensive coordination, communication & process redesign
Requires staffing from other departments?	Yes = 10, No = 0
End user training impact	Rank from 0 – 10: 0 = none, 10 = Classroom with CBT
Budget identified and approved	0 = Available funding by the department, 10 = No funding available

make it easy to do the right thing. For example, if the alert logic finds that there is no advanced directive on the chart, the next step to obtaining one should be queued up for ease-of-ordering. Or if there is a current advanced directive perhaps the next right step is for the provider to be able to access and review it. Regardless of the actual steps involved, building well-conceived, actionable decision logic often takes much more time than assumed.

Taken together, some sense of priority and complexity must translate into an indication of EHR governance capacity. You may need to adjust the aperture on submissions to counterbalance requests from leadership and align with the resources available to operationalize and deploy them. A bottleneck at one or more points in a change request's lifecycle will often trigger unintended delays with other requests, so vigilant tracking is important. Once this starts to happen it can snowball quickly, making a return to normal processes hard.

Voice of the Customer

When launching your governance structure, the source of EHR change requests deserves thoughtful consideration. In my experience there are two different, but passionate, perspectives on this matter. The first group feels that almost all requests should be driven by leadership from the top-down while the second group champions a more decentralized, bottom-up approach. I fall somewhere closer to the latter group, although, logically, some types of requests need to be driven from the top.

Leadership is the voice of the organization and is well-suited to driving change that has broad impact and economic consequences such as quality initiatives, compliance issues, software upgrades, and best practice mandates. Well-meaning administrators have argued that all EHR change requests should be driven from the top-down to promote standardization, but this approach isn't well supported by the informatics literature. If fact, this centralized form of decision-making seems to have the unintended consequences of being paternalistic and disempowering to the provider end users of the system. There is no reason to believe that an administrator who has little or no contact with the EHR or patients has a better understanding of how to manage the EHR than the providers on the front lines using it. Top-down requests should be infrequent, long lasting, and have large and broad economic benefit.

Bottom-up requests are the voice of the end user seeking to improve the physician-patient experience and outcomes by enhancing EHR content, workflow, and connectivity. This decentralized form of decision-making represents innovation and is respectful of the end user's expertise and needs. Bottom-up requests should be frequent, time critical, and interpreted within a specific context (Figure 2.5).

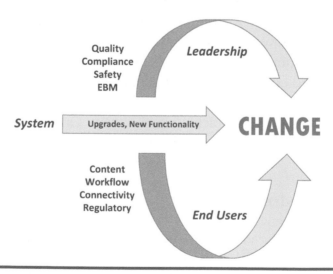

Figure 2.5   In general, changes to the EHR can be driven by leadership from the top-down, by end users from the bottom-up, or through regular system upgrades and new functionality.

When practicing decentralized decision-making, be transparent about how decisions are made and support strategy and processes that bring the decision-making closer to where the work is performed. Empower these end users by making information tools readily available, reward critical thinking and problem-solving skills (Table 2.3).

Table 2.3 Comparison of the Qualities of Centralized and Decentralized Decision-Making.

Centralized	Decentralize
Infrequent – Not made very often and usually not urgent.	**Frequent** – Routine, everyday decisions.
Long lasting – Once made, highly unlikely to change.	**Time critical** – High cost of delay.
Significant economies of scale – Provides large and broad economic benefit.	**Require local information** – Specific and local technology or customer context is required.

Consider that an EHR governance framework that empowers the end user with decision-making authority can be perceived as both forward thinking and threatening. Forward thinking, because who is better qualified than an end user of the system to weigh in on the best design to meet their needs? At the same time, this innovative style of leadership may threaten command-and-control style leaders who are goal-oriented, authoritative, and decisive. Paul Sloane, a well-respected author who speaks extensively on lateral thinking and innovation, contrasts these two leadership styles in detail (Table 2.4).[4]

Although the innovative leadership style immediately resonates as more modern and egalitarian, context is crucial. For example, you probably want your surgical and trauma teams to have a healthy amount of command-and-control leadership. However, it's not a style that will accommodate the continual change and ambiguity that defines EHR governance. If you regularly engage with or report to command-and-control style leaders, you may encounter political tension in the organization as your EHR governance processes mature and scale. We won't spend a great deal of time discussing the best way to handle organizational politics. I suspect that those of you with an interest in this subject already know how to spar in this arena. However, understanding the political machinations within your organization is essential to getting your work done. A decision to engage or not engage in politics should be based on a thorough understanding of the game afoot and the positions of the players. Burying your head in the sand and denying that politics exist makes you and your processes potential victims to those who have chosen to play the game.

Table 2.4 The Command and Control Leader Compared with the Innovative Leader

The Command and Control Leader ...	The Innovative Leader ...
Leads from the front.	Leads from the side.
Directs.	Inspires.
Checks and controls.	Trusts and delegates.
Improves effectiveness and efficiency.	Finds new approaches.
Thinks he knows best (and often does).	Harnesses the abilities of others.
Has a strong sense of direction and purpose.	Has a clear vision and communicates it.
Prioritizes operational over strategic issues.	Prioritizes strategic over operational issues.
Gives directions and orders.	Asks questions and solicits suggestions.
Treats staff as subordinates.	Treats staff as colleagues.
Is decisive, often without prior consultation.	Ponders and solicits input before making decisions.
Builds a team who can execute policy and implement plans.	Builds a team who can create and innovate.
Instructs.	Empowers.
Hires based on experience, track record, and qualifications.	Hires based on attitude, creativity, and latent capabilities.
Discourages dissent.	Encourages constructive dissent.
Cares about results above all.	Cares about ideas, peoples, and the vision.
Promotes himself as the leader and figurehead.	Shares exposure and prestige with the team.
Encourages action, activity, and work.	Encourages ideas, innovation, and fun.
Rewards performance.	Rewards entrepreneurial action.
Is numbers-oriented and analytical.	Is ideas-oriented, analytical, and intuitive.
Sees technology as a means to do things better, faster, and cheaper.	Sees technology as a means to do things entirely differently.
Minimizes risk.	Takes calculated risks.
Abhors failure.	Is comfortable with failure.

Source: Adapted from Paul Sloane, *https://www.destination-innovation.com/*

Chapter Summary

- Establishing governance processes for your EHR is inevitable. The earlier you do this, the better.
- Lack of a governance structure after EHR activation may lead to change request processes that are perceived as unfair or inequitable. This erodes trust.
- Not all change requests need or benefit from governance processes.
- Determine the right balance of top-down and bottom-up change requests for your organization. Centralized decision-making is key for highly standardized changes with broad impact. Decentralized decision-making respects end-user needs and expertise.
- If change request volume becomes a problem, limit the number of requests that can be submitted. Priority and complexity algorithms may be useful in making that determination.
- Be proactive about setting and communicating expectations for change request throughput and turnaround time.

Chapter Exercises

The next step in building your EHR Governance Toolkit is to determine when governance is required and when it is not – in other words, the initial scope of your processes. You may add (and perhaps occasionally remove) things from the scope of your work in the first few years as you scale and refine in response to use cases that you hadn't considered. A general rule of thumb is that if it impacts a provider, governance is appropriate. On day 1, start with those things that have the greatest impact on your end users. Once you've optimized those processes, expand as resources, interest, and support allow.

A few questions to consider as you draft this section:

1. If something is broken in your EHR, what are the steps required to fix it?
2. Do you have a regular (daily?) change control meeting? If yes, what types of requests are handled by this process?
3. How does an end user get a change made in the EHR?
4. How are optimization projects vetted for end-user input?
5. Should EHR updates/upgrades be vetted through governance?
6. Will regulatory changes come through governance (not for a yes/no vote but for design input)?
7. Do you have resources committed to support your proposed EHR governance scope?
8. How will you set expectations regarding the time required to operationalize a change request? Should you adopt a prioritization tool to assess requests? A complexity tool?

Armed with your responses, draft the scope section to your Toolkit. Capture as much detail as possible about the different categories of change requests and how they will be managed (e.g., break/fix, bypass, expert mediated, etc). If you'll be using a priority or complexity scoring tool, be sure to add them into your documentation here.

Chapter 3

How Governance

Would you tell me, please, which way I ought to go from here?

That depends a good deal on where you want to get to, said the Cat.

I don't much care where – said Alice.

Then it doesn't matter which way you go, said the Cat.

– so long as I get SOMEWHERE, Alice added as an explanation.

Oh, you're sure to do that, said the Cat, if you only walk long enough.

– Exchange between Alice and the Cheshire Cat
***Alice in Wonderland*, Lewis Carroll**

Governance Dependencies

In the next section of this book, we take a deep dive into how we unfold EHR governance change processes. However, before walking step-by-step through that, let's shore up a few foundational issues.

The heart of EHR governance is optimizing EHR design. However, EHR design cannot and should not happen in a vacuum. To ensure success, it must be coupled with a define function and a discover function, which we'll refer to as the three Ds (define, design, and discover). Define work is the purview of groups like clinical councils, quality, and others tasked with

DOI: 10.4324/9781003008408-4

maintaining alignment with evidence-based best practice. Discover work is driven by the data science and analytics teams leveraging resources like a data warehouse. Taken together, this iterative, cyclical relationship between these three Ds of define, design, and discover forms the balanced foundation required for lifelong activities in support of a learning healthcare system (Figure 3.1). Let's explore each component in more detail.

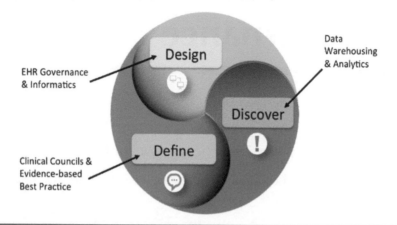

Figure 3.1   A cyclical and interdependent relationship between *defining* best practice, *designing* an elegant interface, and *discovering* insights (the three Ds) that form the balanced foundation required to sustain and support a learning healthcare system.

Design

EHR design work is intended to ensure patient safety, elevate care quality, and achieve the optimal user experience (Figure 3.2).

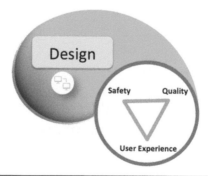

Figure 3.2   The focus of design work is safety, quality, and user experience.

Twenty years ago, the IOM published the landmark report *To Err Is Human*, which reported that somewhere between 44,000 and 98,000 people in the United States die in hospitals each year due to avoidable medical errors.[1] This exceeded deaths from threats such as motor vehicle accidents, breast cancer, and AIDS. The publication sparked an evolution in health-care committed to tackling avoidable medical errors from multiple angles including:

- A focus on creating and sustaining a culture of safety,
- Supporting the healthcare workforce with user-centered design,
- Collaborative partnerships with patients for safe care,
- Leveraging augmented decision support to drive meaningful clinical outcomes, and
- Optimizing health information technology.

While progress has been made with improving certain types of patient safety issues, the ECRI Institute's report on the ten largest patient safety concerns for 2019[2] includes issues directly linked to the use of information technology or those that could be ameliorated if information technology capabilities were better applied. Examples include diagnostic and test result management, antimicrobial stewardship, unregulated apps and mobile devices, siloed behavioral healthcare, and more.

Quality improvement is a well-established practice in a learning healthcare system, and there are several opportunities to merge EHRs with quality improvement throughout all phases of care. For example, EHR systems offer integrated best practice support in the form of clinical decision support, as discussed in some detail in Chapter 1. CDS gives care teams smart, actionable information at the point of care. This improves decision-making by bringing timely information into the workflow exactly when it is needed. It also offers automated functionalities that improve quality and safety through features such as electronic prescribing, drug–drug interaction checking, and drug–allergy interaction checking. For example, one of the electronic clinical quality measures (eCQMs) helps clinicians assess the proportion of their patients with well-controlled hypertension over time. And EHR systems can streamline or even automate data sharing with clinical data registries that use the information to help clinicians choose the best courses of treatment.

While the focus on safety and quality needs no explanation, one may be surprised at the inclusion of the user experience as a principle with equal importance to safety and quality. This is simply because without a low-friction EHR, end-users will devise creative workarounds to reduce experiential pain, all the while inadvertently compromising safety and quality guard rails. Ensuring a superior user experience is one of the most effective ways of supporting patient safety and care quality goals.

I presented on this topic at a national conference where I started the lecture with a series of questions: *When you hear the phrase Electronic Medical Record, what's the first thing that comes to your mind? Hell*, one man close to the front yelled out. Others followed in turn. I showed a Wong-Baker FACES pain rating scale to help audience members self-identify and there was a low level of laughter. Question 2: *What EHR are you on?* Epic, Cerner, Allscripts, Athena Health, Meditech, eClinical-Works, and one name that I'd never heard of before. Last question: *If there was one thing in your EHR you could change, what would it be?* A variety of responses came back including system slowness, poor work-flow, disruption to patient engagement, and better connectivity. One gentleman, an older physician, even piped up and proudly announced that he was still on paper – a rebel in a world full of conformists in the year 2020. Interestingly, not one person currently on an EHR responded that they would go back to paper.

This was consistent with a 2016 study conducted by Deloitte wherein they surveyed a nationally representative sample of US physicians on their attitudes and perceptions about the current market trends impact-ing medicine and future state of the practice of medicine.[3] They reported that although a few physicians would stop using their current EHR system, most wanted improvements. Three of every five surveyed would keep their current EHR and not replace it; 62% wanted interoperability; 57% wanted improved workflow and increased productivity; and 12% were satisfied with the way things were currently.

I finished my lecture with a good 20 minutes remaining for questions, and questions there were. My physician audience had really engaged and were now interested in being heard. They even pushed me to pull out my crystal ball to prognosticate. An ally came to the microphone and talked about how disconnected things were on paper and how much easier and patient-centric the digitized health record world was. My lone provider still on paper chimed in about how smart he was and how his prime objective was to stay on paper until he retired. He cringed when I disagreed with this plan noting that it was a disservice to his patients whose information was inaccessible to other members of their care team. Following the lec-ture, several physicians and one medical student approached. In fact, one physician engaged for a full hour for what I believe was simply an opportunity to vent.

This recent encounter is one of many that continues to convince me that focusing on user experience is key to EHR governance success. Physicians have lived through a great deal of turbulence since 2009 when it comes to EHRs, but a passion still burns in them to get this whole thing right, both for themselves and their patients. A process that focuses exclusively on quality at the expense of user experience will fail. A process that focuses exclusively on safety at the expense of user experience will fail. However, a process that focuses on user experience will also be held to high standards of quality and safety, because users will demand that.

Discover

Discover, the second D, references the ability to aggregate and normalize disparate sources of data into a single place for analysis and insight. Originally the idea of big data was associated with the concepts of volume, variety, and velocity. Current usage, however, refers to the use of advanced data analytics, such as predictive or prescriptive modeling, natural language processing, or machine learning, to extract value from data. Reference to the size of a data set is seldom seen anymore.

In the context of the three Ds, discovery is key to both setting goals for defining work and determining impact from design work. For example, one organization's data insight team analyzed information on severe sepsis over the course of a year for diagnosis-related group (DRG) code 871 (severe sepsis) and concluded that a 10% decrease in length of stay would translate into roughly $10.2 million in savings. Armed with this knowledge, that discovery team worked with both the define and design teams to develop a care pathway to accelerate best practice, improve outcomes, and decrease resource utilization.

The idea of being data-driven has joined the ranks of *innovative, diverse,* and *socially responsible* as one of the most laudable features of organizational culture. Leading with data has become a mandate of many teams, and while there are many opportunities for big data to inform large organizational goals and priorities, there are also two key places directly within EHR governance where data intimately informs process. The first is the data that substantiates the business case being made for a particular change request. The second is the ongoing surveillance of governance process improvement metrics that inform the growth and maturity of your EHR governance. These will be discussed in detail in Chapter 14.

Define

Defining best practice, the final D in our triad, is tightly aligned to the concept of evidence-based medicine (EBM). EBM is a relatively new term that originated with investigators from McMaster's University during the 1990s. However, the concept of EBM was popularized in the mainstream medical literature in 1996, when David Sackett and his colleagues published a landmark editorial in the *British Medical Journal* titled *Evidence based medicine: what it is and what it isn't.*[4] They defined EBM as *the conscientious and judicious use of current best evidence from clinical care research in the management of individual patients.*

The paper continued:

> Evidence based medicine is not "cookbook" medicine. Because it requires a bottom-up approach that integrates the best external evidence with individual clinical expertise and patients' choice, it cannot result in slavish, cookbook approaches to individual patient care. External clinical evidence can inform, but can never replace, individual clinical expertise, and it is this expertise that decides whether the external evidence applies to the individual patient at all and, if so, how it should be integrated into a clinical decision. Similarly, any external guideline must be integrated with individual clinical expertise in deciding whether and how it matches the patient's clinical state, predicament, and preferences, and thus whether it should be applied. Clinicians who fear top-down cookbooks will find the advocates of evidence based medicine joining them at the barricades …
> And if no randomised trial has been carried out for our patient's predicament, we must follow the trail to the next best external evidence and work from there.

To summarize, EBM is the pursuit of the best possible outcome which is informed by three sources of information: research-based evidence (e.g., the medical literature, best practice guidelines), clinical expertise (e.g., clinician's accumulated experience, knowledge, and clinical skills), and patient's values and preferences (Figure 3.3).

Figure 3.3 **The focus of define work is evidence, experts, and patient experience.**

Of the three components, research-based evidence receives the most attention with Sackett's hierarchy of evidence pyramid being recognized by most (Figure 3.4). As analytic methods have matured, this pyramid too has been refined and adapted with greater granularity. At the base we find the weakest form of evidence, background information, and expert opinions. As one ascends the pyramid, the strength of evidence increases with meta-analyses regarded as the highest form of evidence at the peak.

Figure 3.4 **The hierarchy of evidence pyramid organizes clinical research based on study designs.** Source: Adapted from Sackett et al., *BMJ* 1996;312:71.

Today EBM, expressed through guidelines and care pathways, is the very heart of delivering a high standard of care. Evidence-based practice is a form of critical thinking that helps the clinician use EBM effectively and

Figure 3.5   **The five As of the evidence cycle that forms the basis of evidence-based practice. Depicted in a circle to indicate an ongoing process in clinical practice.** Source: Adapted from Richardson et al., *The well-built clinical question: a key to evidence-based decisions*. ACP Journal Club. Nov-Dec 1995; 123: A-12.

efficiently. It is classically comprised of five steps also known as the five As (Figure 3.5):

1. Ask a clinical question.
2. Acquire the best evidence possible.
3. Appraise the evidence, making sure it is applicable to the population or patient.
4. Apply the evidence.
5. Assess the outcome.

Digital innovation and EHRs have played a large role in the advancement of evidence-based practice by making easier work of digesting an ever-growing amount of medical literature. The *Index Medicus* has become a medical dinosaur that today's medical students don't even recognize. The internet has also allowed immediate access to massive amounts of information. However, with the power to access this massive amount of information comes the responsibility to use it wisely. Evidence and data do not immediately translate into evidence-based practice. Even the best EBM has always been intended to augment the medical decision-making process, not replace it.

Software Needs for EHR Governance

To have a successful EHR governance framework, we must also have the appropriate software platforms to support the EHR governance process itself. Generally speaking, there are five platform functions required for EHR governance: (1) a defect tracking tool to manage the change request tickets (e.g., Application Lifecycle Management, Service Now); (2) a document repository with some communication functionality (e.g., SharePoint, Box); (3) a meeting or event platform (e.g., WebEx, Microsoft Teams Meetings); (4) a crowd sourcing and collaboration tool (e.g., Slack, Ryver); and (5) a data analysis and visualization tool (e.g., Tableau, Qlikview). Naturally, email is also a platform used for communication.

Defect Tracking

Being able to submit and track change requests is a primary function of EHR governance. Whatever software you choose to meet this need, take the time to consider the ease of use for those submitting a request, those managing a request, and the ability to draw down data in a structured or free text fashion to track key performance indicators. One team that I worked with inherited a defect tracking software that required several years of modification and refinement to meet the constantly evolving needs of EHR governance processes. We'll discuss the process entailed in submitting a change request ticket, in detail, in the next chapter.

Document Repository

EHR governance processes require a single location where pertinent documents can be organized and stored for easy access. This includes the Toolkit which outlines your EHR governance processes, reference information and forms, charters, meeting agendas, meeting minutes, voting body members, and more.

For example, one organization I worked with had a clinical informatics portal page with nine different icons, one of which linked to the EHR governance page. Here a series of tabs made it easy to navigate to any group managed by EHR governance processes or find governance-related documentation. Take the time early on to settle on a framework that can grow and scale with you as you mature. Going back after the fact to reorganize your filing system can entail a good bit of effort.

Meeting Software

Groups convened to make decisions about EHR governance may be comprised of representatives from geographically distant locations, so an effective virtual meeting and collaboration tool is critical to fostering a sense of common purpose among committee members. Voice-only meetings are not adequate for successful governance meetings. Several software companies offer tools that align with the various processes in the EHR governance framework. Some of the more mature products have a meeting center symbolically equivalent to having all attendees sit at a conference table and consult. This is ideal for planning meetings where open consultation is occurring. In reviewing the membership of the decision-body meetings, one can see that there are specific roles for participants. These roles include some silent observers who attend primarily for learning and information dissemination. In order to achieve this sort of facilitated meeting, other meeting functionality may be more appropriate. For example, an event center functionality mimicks a panel-style discussion where decision-makers and advisors consult, but where other audience members can listen but cannot interrupt.

Collaboration Tool

Over the last seven years, collaboration tools have become wildly popular. Those of us using them wonder how we ever survived without. Simply stated, these tools provide you and your team with one platform that has the efficiency of chat and the clarity of threaded discussions. This includes real-time messaging, file sharing, archiving, and a search function immediately accessible from any connected device. Some of the features used daily for EHR governance processes include:

- Create teams
- Public and private chats
- Posts
- Post stream
- Post reminders
- Global search
- 100% full functionality on all devices
- Integration with popular apps

One team I worked with also created a process to use the collaboration tool to host virtual asynchronous decision-body meetings. We will discuss this in greater detail later in the book. However, the gist is that a framework, much like that of our web-based meetings, was set up on a collaboration platform. Decision-body members then chatted about and voted on change requests asynchronously, at their convenience. It was not unusual to see a comment, for example, from an orthopedic surgeon on the platform time-stamped at 5:20 am or 9:30 pm.

Data Analysis and Visualization Tools

Having software where you can readily analyze and visualize your data is an EHR governance imperative since your immediate success will hinge upon your ability to demonstrate improvement and value. While it may be feasible early on to cobble together your metrics in Excel, your data will quickly become unmanageable and difficult to track reproducibly over time. If possible, choose a data analysis and visualization tool that is flexible and interactive. This adds to the transparency of your EHR governance processes by empowering others to manipulate information from their perspective with a particular question in mind.

Establish an etiquette of labeling your data fields clearly and creating a data dictionary so that anyone working with the information can explain and reproduce the methodology used in defining a specific cohort or metric. Too often, there is a rush to push out results and reports that can't be easily validated or reproduced.

A Roadmap for Leading Change

EHR governance is about change. In the past this meant targeting several large projects and perhaps a few quality goals each year, but now change is continuous and accelerating. Rapidly evolving, disruptive technologies are redefining the need for a robust, responsive change management process. And few things elicit more consternation and emotion from otherwise professional, mild-mannered physicians than the subject of changes to their EHR system.

In a recent Forbes Insights report done with the Project Management Institute, 94% of survey respondents said they faced significant challenges creating a culture of change.[5] Why? The top three challenges cited were, first, that employees see change as a threat to their jobs; second, approaching digital transformation as a technology and not a people issue; and third, the assumption that the culture already promotes constant change. Over the last 12 years, I've experienced much of this first hand.

Transitioning from paper to an electronic system is stressful. Workflows are disrupted, patients are inconvenienced, and the learning curve, for many, is steep.

As a physician informaticist, my skin is thick and my compassion, deep. I've stood in the middle of Medical Executive Committee (MEC) meetings, the object of friendly and not-so-friendly fire. I've had physician colleagues send letters to executive leadership threatening a return to paper orders and documentation. I've had C-suite leaders negotiate vigorously in the ninth hour to keep EHR support teams in place to ensure local resources were comfortable taking the helm.

I fully appreciate that EHR adoption can be a challenge for any individual or organization however, there are few industries as demanding of solid change management processes as healthcare. With patient lives, professional reputations, and billion-dollar brands at stake, changes in healthcare can be intimidating – but also game changing. On several occasions, teams I have worked with have been called in after a first (or sometimes second or third) failed attempt at change. And although many factors can impede change, most failed attempts can be lumped into two categories: poor execution or a non-supportive culture.

Many organizations don't realize that there's a true rigor involved in change management that can and should be embraced when taking on significant change. And there are several change methodologies out there to choose from. Organizations adopting Lean have instantiated a customer-centric culture model focused on continuously improving processes through the elimination of waste whenever and wherever possible. Resources trained in value stream mapping leverage tools such as the plan-do-study-act process to drive process improvement[6] (Figure 3.6).

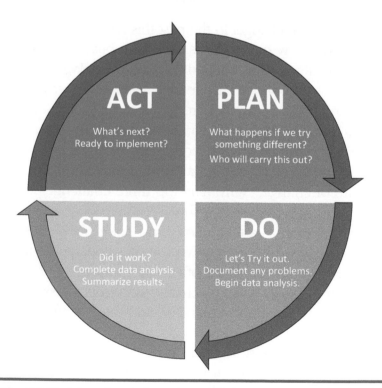

Figure 3.6 **The PDSA (plan-do-study-act) rapid improvement cycle developed by Edward Deming.**

Six Sigma advocates the use of many tools in the Lean toolkit but takes a more analytic tact using the DMAIC (Define, Measure, Analyze, Improve, and Control) improvement cycle as the core framework (Figure 3.7). DMAIC begins with clearly *defining* the problem that needs to be solved, including the scope and timeline. The *measure* step is intended to establish and capture baseline metrics. The *analyze* step is focused on selecting and validating the root cause or causes for elimination. The *improve* step identifies, tests, and implements a solution to the problem. *Control*, the final step in the DMAIC framework, quantifies benefits, tracks improvement, and officially closes the project. DMAIC is not exclusive to Six Sigma and can be used as the framework for other improvement applications.

Figure 3.7   **The Six Sigma DMAIC cycle of process improvement.**

In 1996, Harvard Business School Professor John Kotter forever transformed the way we think about change with his bestselling book, *Leading Change*.[7] Built on the work of Kurt Lewin's unfreeze-change-refreeze model, Kotter set out the eight key steps of the change process, arguing that neglecting any of the steps can be enough for the whole initiative to fail. The first four steps – creating urgency, forming a powerful coalition, creating a vision, and communicating the vision – are intended to unfreeze an existing culture. The next three steps – removing obstacles, creating short-term wins, and building on the change – are meant to make change happen. The eighth and final step – anchoring the change – refreezes the new process within the culture, encouraging it to become part of the status quo.

Step 1: Create Urgency
The ability to change is key to the success of every healthcare organization. Instilling an awareness of existing problems and possible solutions is

powerful and useful in garnering support for change. This can happen, for example, through town hall meetings where information is communicated about what is happening and what direction the organization could go, or through ongoing forums where issues and potential solutions are raised and discussed. Kotter estimates that roughly 75% of a company's management needs to be behind a change for it to be successful, an important point to keep in mind. The key here is to create the *need* for change, not just a desire. The difference between the two cannot be overstated when it comes to the support and eventual success of the change.

Step 2: Form a Powerful Coalition

Change is a team sport, and the thoughtful composition of that team may spell the difference between success and failure. Create a team that can reach out across siloes and break down potential barriers to resistance. This group should be cross-disciplinary and represent a range of experiences and people from different areas of the business to maximize its effectiveness. This coalition will spread messages throughout the organization, delegate tasks, and ensure support for the change organization wide. Team members that collaborate, complement each other, and can drive each other to work harder will increase the likelihood of successful change.

Step 3: Create a Vision for Change

While a change initiative can be complicated and hard to understand, the vision statement for that change must be simple, inspirational, and memorable. It should encapsulate the overall aim in a way that generates support from the whole organization. A great example is Disney's vision statement – *To Make People Happy.*

Step 4: Communicate the Vision

Creating the vision is not enough. To generate support for it, it then needs to be communicated throughout the organization. This is an excellent opportunity to utilize the coalition you have built up, as between them they are likely to have networks in every area of the business. Don't be afraid to share the vision again and again. It cannot be over communicated. Sharing stories and metaphors that exemplify the vision are also powerful ways to be inspirational and have maximum effect.

Step 5: Remove Obstacles

The first four steps are essential in building the strength of your change initiative, but it is also important to look for what is likely to reduce the chances for success. Whether it's individuals, traditions, legislation, or physical obstacles, it is likely there will be a few barriers blocking your pathway to change. Identify these as early as possible and rely on available resources to break them down, without disrupting any other areas of the business.

Step 6: Create Short-Term Wins

Change processes often take a while to reap any rewards, and this can cause support to falter if individuals think their time or efforts have been wasted. You must be able to demonstrate the advantages of the new process by creating some short-term wins. Shorter-term targets are also useful tools for motivation and direction. Using these wins to justify investment and effort can help remotivate staff to continue backing the change.

Step 7: Build on the Change

Change takes time, and many change processes fail over time simply because complacency sets in. The initial momentum, driven by a pressing need, fades while the care and feeding of the project dwindles. Be vigilant by setting goals and analyzing what could be done better for continued improvement. Remember, change is not a destination that one arrives at but rather an ongoing journey of iterative process improvement.

Step 8: Anchor the Changes in Corporate Culture

While execution hurdles can be readily addressed with the steps above, a supportive, motivated culture takes time to build. Without it, engaging staff in change becomes an arduous task that often is less successful and sustainable. Keeping senior stakeholders on board, encouraging new employees to adopt change, and celebrating individuals who adopt new processes will all help weave the change into the DNA of your organization. When done correctly and consistently, each successive change will be smoother.

Change is hard. In fact, Kotter argues that 70% of all change initiatives fail because organizations don't pay attention to the initial work required or fail to maintain the momentum needed to see a process through to its completion. Acknowledging this, the next and largest section of this book is devoted to a deep dive on change. Chapters 4 through 11 discuss each of the eight steps of the *Leading Change* model, applied specifically to EHR governance processes.

Chapter Summary

- EHR governance is focused on design but depends upon a team that defines evidence-based best practice and a team that leverages data and analytics for discovery work.
- Several types of software are required to facilitate EHR governance processes:
  - A defect (change request) tracking tool
  - A document repository
  - A meeting or event platform
  - A crowd sourcing and collaboration tool
  - A data analysis and visualization tool
  - Email
- Change management involves true rigor. A specific methodology should be embraced and followed consistently to obtain the best results with EHR governance processes.

Chapter Exercises

In the next eight chapters of this book, we will dive deeply into the details of how to operationalize EHR governance processes. For this chapter's exercise, let's add a few higher-level *how* items to our EHR Governance Toolkit.

1. What group in your organization is responsible for defining best practice and how do you partner with them?
2. What group in your organization leverages data and analytics for new insights and how do you partner with them?
3. What defect management software tool will you use to track your change requests?* Is this the same tool that change control uses in your organization?
4. Where will you store documents and process documentation?*
5. What meeting or event platform will you use?*
6. What's your communication platform?* Data analysis and visualization tool?*
7. What change management methodology does your organization use? Are there trained resources (e.g., Six Sigma Black Belt) that you can request assistance from?

*Note: Please ensure that you have adequate licenses available for any software that you commit to for your EHR governance processes.

CHANGE

Change will not come if we wait for some other person or some other time. We are the ones we've been waiting for. We are the change that we seek.

– Barack Obama

DOI: 10.4324/9781003008408-5

Chapter 4

Create Urgency

People who bring transformative change have courage, know how to re-frame the problem, and have a sense of urgency.

– Malcolm Gladwell

The Eisenhower Box

EHR governance is about change and successful change begins with a pressing need. In his landmark book *Leading Change*, John Kotter calls this a sense of urgency, while Simon Sinek points to a similar path telling us to *Start with Why*,[1] and the first step of the widely embraced Lean Six Sigma DMAIC methodology[2] is to clearly define the problem. No matter your favorite paradigm, every great leader, change guru, and process engineer knows that the risk of failure is high when you haven't taken the time to clearly articulate the problem you are trying to solve and the compelling reason for solving it. All legendary battles begin with a moral imperative, a pressing need, a call to action. A charismatic leader rallies the troops with the reason for engaging in combat: to preserve freedom; to defend truth, justice, and the American way; to root out an evil. And that reason, that sense of urgency, it does something important. It unifies people in a shared vision, it soothes anxiety, and it empowers correct action.

After finishing a residency in Preventive Medicine and Public Health, I was accepted into an elite epidemiology fellowship at the CDC. As an Epidemic Intelligence Service (EIS) officer within the Division of Nutrition, I worked with the world's experts on iron deficiency anemia and breastfeeding. It was inevitable that I would be infected by these passions, finding myself completely absorbed by the art and science of developing elegant study designs and clearly

DOI: 10.4324/9781003008408-6

articulated problem statements. The epidemiologist's usability principle, *Keep It Simple Stupid* or KISS, became my mantra while the ability to reframe a problem into a 2 × 2 table evoked a sense of accomplishment and honor. Years later, when I learned of the Eisenhower Box, I recognized a kindred spirit in the 34th President of the United States, Dwight D. Eisenhower.

President Eisenhower lived one of the most productive lives you can imagine during his two terms as president from 1953 to 1961. During his time in office, he launched programs that directly led to the development of the Interstate Highway System in the United States, the launch of the internet (Defense Advance Research Project or DARPA), the exploration of space (NASA), and the peaceful use of alternative energy sources (Atomic Energy Act). Before becoming president, Eisenhower was a five-star general in the United States Army, served as the Supreme Commander of the Allied Forces in Europe during World War II, and was responsible for planning and executing invasions of North Africa, France, and Germany. At other points along the way, he served as President of Columbia University, became the first Supreme Commander of NATO, and somehow found time to pursue hobbies like golfing and oil painting. Eisenhower had an incredible ability to sustain his productivity not just for weeks or months, but for decades. And for that reason, it is no surprise that his methods for time management, task management, and productivity have been studied by many people. His most famous productivity strategy, the Eisenhower Box (or Eisenhower Matrix), is a simple decision-making 2 × 2 table (Figure 4.1).

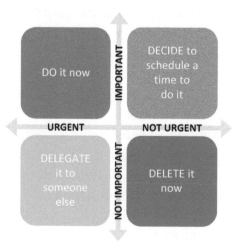

Figure 4.1   The Eisenhower Box is a 2×2 table where urgency (urgent/not urgent) is mapped horizontally, and importance (important/not important) is mapped vertically. This allows for the rapid recognition of high-priority issues.

A 2 × 2 table is a compact summary of data for two variables. For the Eisenhower Box, urgency (urgent/not urgent) is mapped horizontally, and importance (important/not important) is mapped vertically. The value of plotting activities this way is that you can quickly see what activities fall into each of the four quadrants and prioritize your time accordingly. You'll do this in an exercise at the end of this chapter using the list that you created in Chapter 1.

Urgency is triggered by two things: opportunity and anxiety.[3] Opportunity generates a momentum that matures the organization in a positive direction and sustains itself over time. Purpose creates synergy for opportunity. It taps into what is meaningful and important helping people fight their natural inclination to resist change and come along. Anxiety is fear-based and while it may overcome inertia for a short period of time, it cannot generate or sustain momentum. Instead, it usually leads to panic, stressing people out and eventually saps the organization of the very spirit it so desires to generate. We've all seen both opportunity-driven urgency and anxiety-driven activity in action. However, to create change of real significance, to execute any new and different strategy, you need a sense of true opportunity-driven urgency among as many people as possible. Kotter warns that unless 50%–70% of managers and employees feel a compelling need to change, failure looms. He recommends four ways to increase the urgency needed for change.[4]

First, *listen to the people on the front line – go to the gemba* (gemba is a Japanese term in the Lean lexicon meaning *the actual place*). Go out and observe what is really happening while showing respect to the people involved. Who knows better than the practitioners using the EHR, whether it is a useful and usable tool? Providers, nurses, mid-levels, pharmacists, and the like – the primary customers and consumers of the EHR – are the best source of information on what works well and what would benefit from improvement. Some of the world's most successful entrepreneurs rely on this method with great success. They regularly visit offices, stores, and factories and ask frontline employees questions about customers and customer reaction to their products or services. They listen carefully and look for patterns and encourage other managers to do the same. They encourage or require that frontline supervisors engage in some form of this activity as an ongoing part of their jobs. Sam Walton was a prominent example of someone who used this practice, and Walmart, during his years, was the most successful organization of its kind in the world. The same was true for Herb Kelleher at Southwest Airlines. Bring back new information about your EHR system and a newfound determination to do something meaningful with it.

Second, *show them, don't tell them*. At one time or another, we've all encountered someone who said something that was inconsistent with what they did. When faced with this type of discordance we naturally gravitate toward believing actions over words; the phrase *actions speak louder than words* resonates well with us. Herein lies the power in showing people. Tell stories that are honest and human. Show videos. Strive to move beyond sanitized facts and data to people and emotions. Seek to capture hearts and minds in support of the cause. And above all, be the change you want to see.

Third, *allow the data to anger you, then it can set you free*. Leaders often shy away from disturbing data worried that it will unsettle people. They believe most people are not smart enough or experienced enough to understand it or that the information will damage morale, increase anxiety, and lead to increased turnover. However, this need not be the case. Framed as a challenge in need of a solution, disturbing data can be a strong and compelling catalyst to unify the masses around change.

Never assume that the people you're leading or working with see what you see, even if a problem or opportunity seems obvious, blazing, or impossible to miss. People's view of the world is limited by silo walls and the ceilings and doors of their level in the hierarchy. A few emails or town hall meetings will not change this. And so-called burning platforms can create more problems than solutions. Think of a crowded movie theater. Before yelling *fire!* consider the risk of people being trampled to death trying to exit the theater or consider that even if they do make it out alive, they'll probably run frantically in ten different directions before collapsing, exhausted. No organization needs that kind of negative energy. Likewise keep in mind that when it comes to sustained effort at a high level, positive feelings are infinitely more successful than negative. Fear and anxiety produce adrenaline which keeps people going for a limited time before leading quickly to burnout. So always share the data – good, bad, or otherwise – in a way that frames it as an opportunity for improvement.

Solution Jumping

Leaders enjoy solving problems. In fact, we are promoted and make more money for our problem-solving skills giving us a naturally reinforced tendency to solution jump. There are times, especially when an issue is framed as urgent, when we don't spend enough time making sure that the problem we are solving is ours to solve nor do we always validate that the problem identified is the right problem. Sometimes we think we've identified the root cause of a problem and rush to call in a swarm of professionals to solve it, only to find out that we were wrong in the root cause assumption, failed to frame the problem, and jumped to a solution. Recently I did just that.

A colleague invited me into an ongoing series of meetings regarding a bug in our EHR software that was believed to be creating a potential patient safety issue. Empowered by a sense of urgency, in good faith, I acted quickly. However, I failed to adequately frame the problem well enough to understand that the impact of my solution differed in the inpatient and outpatient environment with unintended consequences for many providers that could have been avoided. Realizing this afterwards, the team and I spent the next two weeks refining the solution and performing a root cause analysis to identify safeguards that would prevent this type of solution jumping going forward.

Solution jumping is your brain thinking too fast. When considering a problem, especially a problem presented with a certain amount of urgency, your brain digests sound bites while filling in the empty space to create a coherent story that makes sense. That story is then used to support a solution that it feels certain will work. Approaching a problem from your unique perspective alone is a form of cognitive bias known as the *expertise trap*. This narrow mindset limits the tools that can be brought to bear in problem-solving. Abraham Maslow, who is famous for his hierarchy of needs model, called this the law of the instrument. Basically, he said if the only tool that you have in your toolkit is a hammer, everything looks like a nail. The point he was making was that if, for example, you're a lawyer and your toolkit is the toolkit of torts and legal precedents, then you're going to see all problems through that very narrow lens.

The answer is to slow down and be more deliberate and structured in understanding the problem that needs solving. Corey Phelps, coauthor of *Cracked It: How to Solve Big Problems and Sell Solutions like Top Strategy Consultants*, recommends applying a consistently methodical approach to complex problem-solving:[5] step 1 is to state the problem. Specifically answer the question, *what is the problem I am trying to solve?* Step 2 is to frame the problem. Give it context and start looking at potential causes of the problem. In the 2017 *Harvard Business Review* article *Are You Solving the Right Problems?*[6] author Thomas Wedell-Wedellsborg, speaking to the leader's penchant for quickly moving into problem-solving mode, offers seven practices for reframing problems:

1. Establish legitimacy. Share the technique and supporting information so people take it seriously.
2. Bring outsiders to the discussion. This is the single most important tool for reframing a problem. Find people who understand your world but are not part of your world and ask them for feedback and input, not solutions.
3. Get your stakeholders to define the problem in writing. Remove names and ask for full sentences (not just bullet points) so you can better understand context and perspective.
4. Simply ask people what is missing. Often people won't share this information, for fear of sounding critical, unless asked.
5. Have people identify what category of problem they think something is.
6. Analyze the times when the problem did not occur. What was different about that situation?
7. Make sure you have a clearly articulated, agreed-upon objective. Sometimes people may be solving different problems.

The third step, the step most leaders are rather skilled at, is generating solutions. And the final step, number four, is to test and evaluate the solutions. This real-world proof of concept is critical since it is impossible to figure it all out from within the comfy confines of your office. Go out to meet with the people actually experiencing the problem and prototype your ideas.

The tools you use to prevent solution jumping can and should feel messy and confusing at times. The more you do it, the easier it gets. So, if like me you find yourself drawn into solving a problem before you've adequately defined it, use one of the methods above to pause and reframe. Doing this at the beginning will save you the time required to do it over. Remember, while you may feel a sense of urgency pushing you, the speed of a response is far less important than the precision of that response.

The Case for a Good Business Case

A change request with a well-articulated business case and supporting data helps to evaluate urgency and is a key to improving the effectiveness and efficiency of EHR governance. Prior to reengineering this process, large amounts of time were wasted clarifying the scope of the problem, the reason for the request, whether there was supporting data for the request, whether the request was technically feasible and exchanges with the builders regarding the design. At times it took over a year for a relatively straightforward request to be completed. Overhauling this process is one of the first things you should consider if your change request process lacks transparency and has become frustrating to all involved. Let's dive into the process one team I worked with created.

After logging into the defect management software, the new defect function was used to create a change request template with a unique ticket number assigned. The screen defaulted to the *Details* tab which is where the majority of the data fields required for a new change request submission existed. Required fields included information such as a title, business case, and source of the request. These required fields, identified by red text, needed to be completed before a change request ticket could be submitted (Figure 4.2). This included a series of structured data fields that captured a descriptive title, the requestor's name, the region the request came from, user affected, care setting, solution module, change justification, release type, validators, and more.

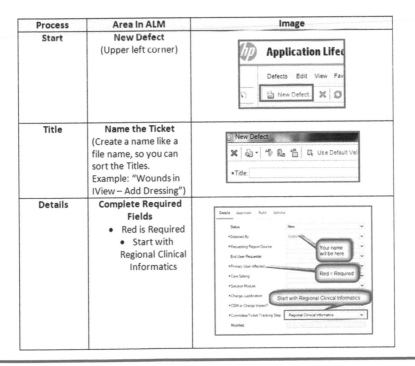

Process	Area In ALM	Image
Start	New Defect (Upper left corner)	
Title	Name the Ticket (Create a name like a file name, so you can sort the Titles. Example: "Wounds in IView – Add Dressing")	
Details	Complete Required Fields • Red is Required • Start with Regional Clinical Informatics	

Figure 4.2 The first three steps for entering an EHR change request into one type of defect management software. Each step is clearly explained with an accompanying image.

A business case, comprised of five short narrative sections (Figure 4.3), was also required in the *Details* tab for each change request. Here clarity mattered and brevity was encouraged. If the business case provided the necessary information to empower the decision maker and the decision-making process, it served its purpose well.

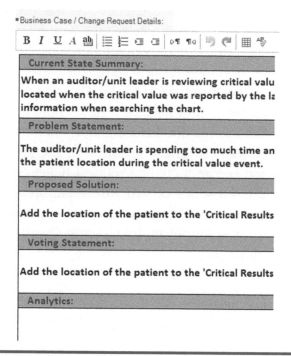

Figure 4.3   An example of the five components required for a complete business case within a change request ticket.

- Section 1: Current State Summary – How the design, workflow, or process existed at the time of the request.
- Section 2: Problem Statement – A brief claim that describes the issue the end user is experiencing and needs solved. This might include an opportunity to generate revenue, cut costs, or deliver benefit; compliance with a required mandate; alignment with new best practice standards; correction of wrong information; or opportunities for enhancements or optimization.
- Section 3: Proposed Solution – The change envisioned to solve the problem. This could be and often was refined by additional technical and design input.
- Section 4: Voting Statement – A clear, concise summary of the requested change in a yes or no format that is written in an easy to understand, non-technical manner.

■ Section 5: Analytics – Data or evidence, reflective of evidence-based best practice, in support of the business case. This could be quantitative, qualitative, or descriptive data. Early on this was desired, encouraged, and praised – but not required. As data capabilities matured, it evolved into a requirement for certain types of requests (e.g., clinical decision support rules).

Files could be attached to each unique change request. This feature was used to capture and associate intake tools, refine business cases, and provide mockups of the requested change (Figure 4.4).

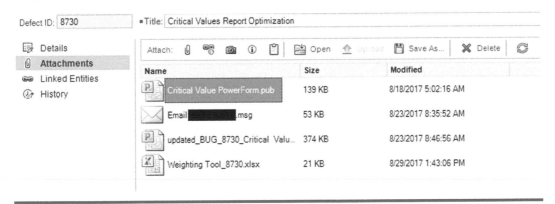

Figure 4.4 **The attachments section within one type of change request software allows multiple supporting documents to be associated with a specific ticket.**

The *Approvals* tab was used to disposition a ticket for decision-body voting (Figure 4.5). A gatekeeper group tasked with reviewing all tickets for completeness and technical feasibility updated the fields in this tab to

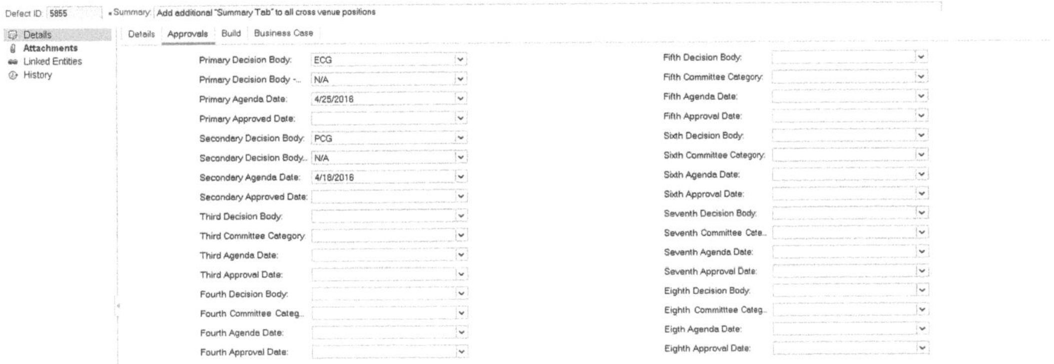

Figure 4.5 **The approvals tab within one type of change request software where the change request is dispositioned to one or multiple decision-making bodies.**

indicate which group or groups needed to see it. This information was used by meeting coordinators to generate decision-body meeting agendas. After voting occurred, this tab was updated with the voting results. Once all decision bodies had voted, the ticket was either approved and moved forward for resourcing or dismissed. The comments section on the *Details* tab was updated accordingly to ensure thorough communication of voting-body decisions.

The *Build* and *Actions* tabs were used by the builders and communications team to track the change request through build and testing in both the test and live environments as well as release and education (Figure 4.6).

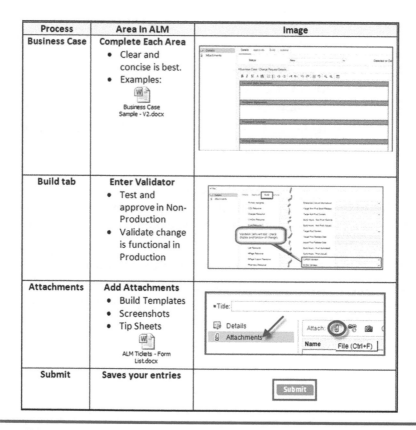

Figure 4.6 **The remaining four steps required to enter a change request ticket into one type of defect management software. Each step is clearly explained with an accompanying image.**

As your EHR and governance processes mature, your change requests will become more complex. When this happens, congratulations are in order – you are maturing toward EHR 3.0. Vigilance is paramount to stay in lock step with your build and communication resources regarding their capacity to keep pace with what is being requested. You may have the same number of requests coming through your processes, but their complexity will create a backlog with build and deployment. Formally gathering key stakeholders every six to eight weeks to review throughput and dashboard metrics will maintain process alignment and help keep you ahead of major issues.

Chapter Summary

- There needs to be opportunity-driven urgency in creating the momentum behind your EHR governance processes.
- Anxiety-based urgency can generate short-term momentum but will not mature the organization in a positive direction and is not sustainable.
- Increase the urgency needed for change by:
  - Listening to the people on the front line; going out and observing what is really happening.
  - Leading by example using stories and videos.
  - Sharing the data – good, bad, or otherwise – in a way that frames it as an opportunity for improvement.

- Don't allow urgency to lead to solution jumping. Apply a consistently methodical approach to complex problem-solving.
- A well-defined change request, which includes a complete business case, provides the information needed to assess the urgency of a given change request.

Chapter Exercises

1. In Chapter 1, you defined the *why* of your EHR governance processes. Now you will take the clarity you honed there and translate it
   into a call to action that can rally others to your cause. Grab a piece
   of paper, draw a large rectangle, and divide it into four equally sized
   quadrants. Label the first column *urgent* and the second column *not
   urgent*. Label the first row *important* and the second row *not important*. Now go ahead and take the list of reasons that you created at the
   end of Chapter 1 for why EHR governance processes were important
   and sort them into one of the four quadrants. The urgent/important
   tasks that fall into the upper left quadrant are your pressing reasons for
   EHR governance; the things you want to focus on now; that will evoke
   passion and drive change. The non-urgent/important tasks that fall into
   the upper right quadrant don't require immediate action but should be
   scheduled for attention in the near future. The urgent/not important
   tasks in the lower left corner can be delegated for follow-up and the
   not urgent/not important tasks in the remaining quadrant should be
   deleted.

   Eisenhower Box Exercise

	Urgent	Not Urgent
Important		
Not Important		

   Who will you collaborate with to communicate the urgency of these
   important issues to generate momentum for your EHR governance
   processes? Remember, your goal is to have 50%–70% of managers and
   employees feel a compelling need to change.
2. Identify what methodology you will use to prevent solution jumping
   and add that documentation to your EHR Governance Toolkit.
3. In Chapter 3, you identified what defect management software you
   were going to use for change request tickets. Now, identify what
   fields will be required on that intake and the components required
   for a complete business case. Feel free to adopt or refine the
   examples provided in the chapter or create something new. Add this
   documentation to your EHR Governance Toolkit.

Chapter 5

Form a Powerful Coalition

Never doubt that a small group of thoughtful citizens can change the world.

Indeed, it is the only thing that ever has.

– Margaret Mead, American cultural anthropologist

It's a Team Sport

Leadership is the lynchpin of a successful EHR governance model. Although the voice and choice model espoused in this book typically associates EHR governance with physician leadership, a greater cast of individuals is required. In other words, physician leadership is *necessary but not sufficient* for EHR governance. What you're looking to develop is a guiding coalition comprised of skilled, credible, influential leaders and managers from across the organization empowered to keep change processes on track and counter organizational resistance. Now perhaps you are shaking your head thinking this sounds unrealistic and quite undoable for a smaller stand-alone hospital, but it simply requires creativity.

Immediately after being hired as the CMIO at my local community hospital, I found myself attending a 30-minute safety huddle meeting every morning. Shortly before 7:30 am leaders and managers from across the hospital descended upon the library to sit down together and discuss any new problems arising in the last 24 hours and receive updates on existing

DOI: 10.4324/9781003008408-7

issues in process. Hosting responsibilities rotated between many members of the C-suite including the COO, CMO, CNO, CIO, CFO, and, at times, the CEO. But even if a senior leader wasn't hosting, they were usually still in attendance. This was part of a *just culture* initiative that the organization had committed to, and the message was clear – this was a top priority. The huddle was an open-door meeting, so it was not unusual for a physician to drop in unannounced with a concern in need of a solution. As part of this culture of safety, my boss, the CIO, would also round on the clinical floors most afternoons where he would usually cross paths with the COO who observed a similar etiquette. Everyone in the organization was aware of these daily morning huddles and smiled at the administrators emerging from their executive suite offices to make clinical rounds. However, these brief morning gatherings and high-visibility afternoon rounds shifted expectations and culture. A small amount of the right people's time created powerful change within the organization. Let's translate that experience into the creation of our guiding coalition for EHR governance.

In the prior chapter, we discussed the unequivocal necessity for inspiring a sense of urgency in creating or refining an EHR governance process. In a like manner, the members of your guiding coalition are an unspoken message that either supports or nullifies that priority. Well-meaning individuals and weak committees rarely gain the momentum or respect required to drive lasting change. Your coalition must be a diverse array of credible, enthusiastic change agents who have the time and power to set a vision and remove obstacles.

This group conveys passion, purpose, and knowledge that engenders trust and inspires others to go above and beyond to get the job done. For example, when I joined a large enterprise health system as their Medical Director of Informatics, I chaired the two largest physician decision-body governance groups, each with 50–70 provider participants from across eight geographically distant regions in the organization. My boss spent a good deal of time onboarding me to make sure I understood the organization's EHR governance values of voice, choice, transparency, and accountability that I was meant to champion and grow. Although I chaired these meetings, I didn't vote (unless there was a 50–50 split that needed a deciding vote) and I didn't veto, by design. I was meant to lead by driving consensus and offering subject matter expertise. My clinical experience, informatics training, and reputation within the organization helped me quickly establish my credibility. Committee members appreciated that I would continue to protect the core values established by my boss before me while offering the skills to approach and assist with problem-solving from multiple angles, in a credible fashion.

If credibility is the foundation of a high functioning coalition, power is the glue. That is, the coalition must have the authority to make decisions that fast-track changes or remove obstacles – prudently, judiciously – when required. Without this, EHR governance will struggle to establish and maintain trust with its constituents when challenging issues requiring tailored solutions inevitably arise. Consider a change request submitted in response to an identified safety event. Here time is of the essence to optimize and approve the design, build, and test it in a non-production environment and then deploy it into the live EHR environment with appropriate communication. To do this, established governance processes and queues may need to be circumvented or bypassed.

What a guiding coalition is is just as important as what a guiding coalition isn't. A few people from various leadership teams sitting around a table together at corporate meetings making decisions isn't a guiding coalition. A guiding coalition does not delegate responsibility; it takes responsibility. And most of all, a guiding coalition does not abide by the status quo. It thinks outside-of-the-box and explores new ways to meet the ever evolving needs of EHR governance. This oversight team for change brings expertise, energy, and perspective across a variety of areas, and peers respect their professionalism.

When pulling together your EHR governance guiding coalition, seek diversity. Aim for inclusive representation from all key groups that have a stake in EHR governance processes. Ideally there should be a mix of management and non-management members who are well connected throughout the organization. While this can add up to quite a few people, the right kinds of people working together make for a more powerful change engine. This may feel daunting but don't be afraid to start with representation from the core groups who are most impacted and then ask for their assistance and recommendations to refine the coalition composition over time. Obtaining a commitment of someone's time often becomes easier after you've had some initial success with your processes.

Behavior is an essential ingredient to coalition success; avoid naysayers, nihilists, and narcissists. Shooting down creative suggestions prevents the coalition from innovating and growing. Unfocused individuals can take the coalition off course when unwavering attention is required to get the job done. And coalition members with hidden agendas will derail efforts and cause the coalition to lose credibility. That being said, a good balance of backgrounds and personalities within the coalition will foster an even perspective; a variety of introverts, extroverts, and unconventional thinkers will usually result in a robust engagement.

There are potential barriers to standing up a guiding coalition that deserve thoughtful consideration. Teams may be sensitive about sharing their work or resources with others. These turf issues may extend to who takes credit or blame for coalition-driven outcomes. To manage this, you will need to be prepared to explain and defend the benefits of working together for the betterment of the larger organization. There may also be a prior history of poor collaboration between individuals or teams that overshadows any new or future collaboration. A new coalition will need to contend with this history if there is any hope of working together. It is not uncommon, especially in a healthcare organization, to have leaders with advanced degrees feel it is their job to rush in and problem-solve. Encouraging an atmosphere of participation and moderating those who feel they have all the answers is almost always part of a new coalition dynamic. Funding is an obvious obstacle as are any conditions that may be attached to allocated resources for EHR governance, generally speaking. Finally, a successful coalition demands collaborative leadership. This may require bringing in an outside facilitator or the internal training of an existing member of the group. Regardless, standing up a new guiding coalition without this skill set poses a major risk.

Occasionally I get asked my opinion about whether physicians participating in EHR governance functions should be paid for their time. If the money is available, that is certainly ideal. However, money wasn't always the most important type of compensation the providers I worked with were seeking. Several organizations I worked with were quite large and employed several full-time physicians at the national and regional levels dedicated to medical informatics. There were also several regional or local physicians who had informatics responsibilities included as part of the administrative time built into their contracts. However, I was always humbled by the physicians who, without contractual obligation or monetary incentive, chose to engage with nothing more than the desire to make things better. They rightly demanded that their time be used effectively and efficiently and that they see results. The literature points to three factors that play a key role in this phenomenon: autonomy, mastery, and purpose.

Autonomy is the engagement of self with a desire to direct one's own destiny. To foster autonomy, you need to allow for self-direction. True autonomy as a motivator, is the perception that you are not being micro-managed and have the ability to make your own decisions without having to seek approval. Recognizing the providers' voice and empowering them to refine their EHR creates a level of autonomy and is a key driver of satisfaction.

Mastery is about seeing progress and is reinforced by sharing results. This desire to see improvement contributes to our inner satisfaction and is not usually financially motivated. In fact, there are current business models where people do highly skilled work for free, volunteering their time up to 30 hours a week, and then they give away what they create rather than sell it (Linux, Apache, Wikipedia). These well-educated people with well-paying jobs are doing equally challenging work in their spare time for free because they are motivated by the challenge of mastery and making a contribution. To invoke the power of mastery, align people with their potential. If a job is too difficult, it will become overwhelming, and if it is too easy, it will become boring. The trick is to provide a compelling challenge in a well-organized, supportive environment.

Purpose is the desire to work with the goal of serving something larger than yourself. This is easier to do when you care about the outcome. In the case of physicians volunteering to participate in EHR governance groups, the commitment was to create a better user experience for themselves, their colleagues, and their patients. If outcomes weren't seen, they would often resign from a group or simply forgo attending the meetings. Well aware of this, governance meetings were facilitated, well-organized, crisp group engagements where results and accomplishments were reported on a regular basis.

We're in This Together

Your guiding coalition can be a group or it can be a team. What's the difference between the two you ask? A group is a collection of individualistic thinkers engaged in problem-solving. They may be in the same room or same virtual meeting together, but they don't share a single vision. Teams, on the other hand, are a synergistic unit of collective performance unified in achieving a common goal. In this way, a team is bigger than the sum of its parts. This kind of commitment requires a driving purpose in which team members can believe. That team spirit and dynamic is the secret to establishing robust EHR governance.

In 2014, the CEO of one organization that I worked with gathered his senior leadership team together to pose a pressing challenge – how do we improve our provider's experience with their EHR? Complaints of longer workdays, burdensome documentation, and disrupted patient engagement were being reported. Providers, eager to solve these problems, voiced concerns that they felt weren't being heard; and even when they were heard, change was slow and painful. The Chief Health Information Officer led the charge armed with a clear directive and a commitment of resources. He first convened a few key people including a project manager, a facilitator, and a clinical informaticist to clarify the charter, rationale, and performance challenge, while leaving sufficient flexibility to reframe the problem, innovate, set goals, timing, and approach. The next step was to conduct focus groups with key stakeholders to perform root cause analyses and process mapping exercises. This is how the initial scope of work was determined, siloes were broken down, and collaborative partnerships between the members of a guiding coalition were formed.

This early discovery work made it clear, quickly, that the best way to tackle these problems with the EHR was to focus on the needs of its primary consumers delivering care at the bedside – the physicians, nurses, midlevels, and others. A partnership between those providers and the future guiding coalition was the beginning of creating a trusted brand; an approach that could be counted upon to be consistent, fair, equitable, and accountable. This then parlayed into a feeling of mutual interdependence and trust – *we are in this together.* I share your concerns, you share my concerns, and together we have a joint commitment to acting in the best interests of the physician–patient relationship. This collegial rapport provides the goodwill required to weather the difficulties that will inevitably arise in the maturation of any EHR.

On March 7, 2018, our EHR vendor notified its clients that it had uncovered a software defect which was summarized as follows: *When you have multiple patient charts open, the active chart can unexpectedly change from one patient to another.* The potential patient safety implications of the defect left no option but to limit providers to single chart access until a software fix was found. With less than 24 hours of notice providers, acknowledging the issue and embracing a shared commitment toward patient care, altered their workflows to accommodate the change. Yes, I received a few emails telling me how inconvenient it was to work limited to one chart access, but it was always prefaced with an understanding of why this action was needed. Two weeks later, when the concern was resolved, their previous multiple chart privileges were restored.

In the absence of a shared commitment in governance, it becomes easier for the *EHR-as-enemy* mentality to take hold. The EHR becomes the default cause for many, if not all the problems experienced by a provider. To offer perspective, Auerbach and colleagues[1] suggest dividing EHR-associated problems into two categories: those created by the EHR and preexisting problems that were made more visible by the EHR.

In the former category, we see that digitizing health records has led to a tsunami of unfiltered data that, so far, remains largely unusable. The ability to autopopulate notes with both structured fields and free text has resulted in unruly, bloated documentation that obscures the patient's story. Providers are beholden to mouse clicks and keystrokes leaving less time for eye contact and personal engagement. And the burden imposed by low-value documentation to meet regulatory, compliance, and quality metrics can add hours of additional work to the already long workday.

In a humorous yet provocative opinion piece *I, EHR,*[2] Indira Sriram and colleagues remind us that the EHR is merely a piece of software and suggest four ways to leverage it to better facilitate physician–patient engagement:

1. Introduce the patient to the EHR and consider taking the patient on a tour.
2. When appropriate, don't hesitate to stop, listen, and make eye contact.
3. Use the EHR as an education and shared decision-making tool. Let the patient review their X-ray and lab results with you.
4. Use the tool to reimagine the patient–physician relationship. Add a picture. Capture personal information that allows for a more intimate engagement.

Existing problems made more visible by the EHR include limitations in quality improvement (QI) tools that have always constrained the scope of QI interventions. What may be different in the EHR era is the expectation that simple changes in the EHR could and would lead to instant changes in care quality. While EHRs are a key part of QI, they are not the first or sole part of an improvement strategy.

A second problem, one of healthcare's own making, is EHR complexity. Requests for flexibility and the desire to respond to the many ways providers work result in difficult-to-maintain customization and variation. It's not unusual to see battle lines drawn between safe, highly reliable (evidence based, standardized) decision-making and what a provider wants because it is what she has always done.

Finally, the EHR makes tasks explicit and auditable. In general, this is a good thing and necessary if one hopes to optimize safety and quality. The key is to make it easy to do the right thing while allowing each member of the care team to operate within their stated policies at the top of their license. For example, the EHR eliminated the rubber stamp that staff used for the physician's signature in the paper world and replaced it with a results review process that could not be delegated. To be physician-friendly, results review needed to be smart enough to flag abnormalities for attention while not being onerous and time consuming. The privileges and preferences of various roles provisioned to use the EHR must reflect workflows under optimized policy so, for example, medical assistants can continue to coordinate seamless ambulatory care.

EHR governance driven by a strong guiding coalition reframes the *EHR-as-enemy* mentality and offers a process for making the EHR a vehicle for innovation, improvement, and standardization – not just technological enhancements. Focus on what people do, what they need to do, and how to leverage smart design, rules, and decision support that allows everyone to practice at the top of their license.

As I mentioned earlier, I was the physician lead for several large EHR go lives. But even in go lives when I wasn't directly engaged as part of the project team, I'd show up for a few weeks to support my colleagues at-the-elbow. This role was key, not so much for any technical knowledge of the EHR build I might have, but for my ability to engage my peers in problem-solving and reassure them that everything was going to be fine. When possible, I liked covering the evening shift. It was satisfying to review the various reports with the command center analysts at night and tie up any loose ends from the day. On one such evening, day one of a large hospital go live, an analyst approached me with a report indicating that several patients were admitted to the hospital without being properly converted from an ED status to an inpatient status. What this meant, effectively, was that all the admission orders for each patient needed to be reentered into the EHR. No small task. Of course it was 11:30 pm by the time we were able to confirm the nature and scope of the problem. I called the admitting hospital physician who promptly informed me that his shift ended in 30 minutes and that this was a problem for his colleague who would be taking over at midnight. I met with both physicians in the ED a few minutes later to discuss how to best solve the problem. Both pointed to the other for accountability in correcting the matter. I informed them that while I could secure assistance with the work at hand, we would *all* be staying together in the ED until the problem was corrected. Not pleased with my solution, they threatened to call the hospital's Chief Medical Officer. Since it was already a few minutes after midnight, that call never happened and we all worked diligently until a little after 2:00 am to correct the matter.

I'm sure everyone has their stories of physicians, normally gracious and empathetic by nature, turning snarky when faced with the inevitable challenges of adopting an EHR. The learning curve can be steep for the new user and, at least initially, it takes more time to get the same amount of work done. New workflows, even when carefully mapped, can burden the physician with low-value activities such as additional documentation requirements. Fortunately, much of this gets resolved during go live, but it doesn't usually disappear completely as evidenced by the parking lot list of optimization and enhancement requests that get handed off when the go-live command center closes. Physicians continue to have skin in the game from both a liability and usability perspective. With this in mind, any coalition guiding EHR governance must include well-respected physicians with physician-impacting decisions being driven by physician consensus. Members of the physician tribe relate to each other's frustrations having all traversed the same rites of passage before being entrusted with the responsibilities of patient care. This unspoken bond confers a joint commitment of respect, support, and service to one another.

Before we conclude this section, let's spend a few moments discussing consultants. Building a guiding coalition that will grow your EHR governance structure is challenging work that requires commitment and consistency over a long period of time. Hiring a consultant skilled in change management and the development of strategic alliances may be exactly what you need to bring a fresh perspective. However, it is *key* that she/he train your core team leaders to be the face of your EHR governance processes and to take the reins of your governance framework out of the gate. This strengthens the fragile proposition on which to build a culture of credibility and trust over the long horizon.

Try To See It My Way

My husband, a hospice and palliative medicine physician, first introduced me to the concept of naïve realism. Although I don't remember the context of the conversation, I feel certain I was going on at the end of a long day, frustrated by a variety of disparate opinions around some problem whose solution was elusive.

He smiled, applying his soothing magic, and explained that naïve realism is the human tendency to believe that we see the world around us objectively and that people who disagree with us must be uninformed, irrational, or biased.[3] I laughed at the wisdom of this truism and shared a joke regarding differing perspectives of an EHR go live that seemed an apt example:[4] the CIO says *that was complicated*, the CMIO thinks *that was cool*, the CMO says *that was disruptive*, the provider thinks *that hurt*, and the CFO complains *that was really expensive*. With this knowledge of naïve realism in hand, the task of developing a cohesive guiding coalition becomes an even greater challenge. This is where the proper understanding and application of tools like reflective listening and persuasion become invaluable.

I first learned about reflective listening during my residency training and years later I found myself teaching it to medical students as part of their preventive medicine curriculum. Many of my students were quick to tell me, in a somewhat dismissive manner, that reflective listening is obvious and simplistic. Years later I grinned whenever I received an email from one of those students, now responsible for patient care, championing reflective listening as a useful tool. The steps involved in reflective listening are straightforward intellectually but take practice to apply practically:[5]

1. Reduce distractions so you can focus upon the conversation.
2. Truly embrace the speaker's perspective, trying to understand its origin, even (especially) if you don't agree with it. Refrain from judgment and offer empathy so others feel at ease speaking freely.
3. Mirror the speaker's mood both in what you say and your non-verbal cues. To do this successfully, you must quiet your mind so you can pay close attention to the smallest details about the speaker: tone of voice, posture, body language, etc. In a world engaged in more and more virtual forms of communication, you'll need to sharpen and trust your intuition at times. The listener will look for congruence between words and mood.
4. Summarize what the speaker said, using the speaker's own words rather than merely paraphrasing words and phrases. This *reflecting back* of essential concepts to the speaker demonstrates your attentiveness and engagement.
5. Respond to the speaker's specific point, without digressing to other subjects. Refrain from idle chatter.

I applied these principles in the EHR governance committees I chaired, which met virtually for one to two hours most weeks. As tempting as it was to multitask, especially when engaged in a virtual meeting where no one can see you doing other things, I tried to turn off everything that wasn't relevant to the meeting at hand. This meant leaving my email, text messaging, and communication platforms active so people could communicate with me behind the scenes. This allowed me to track the pulse of the meeting through others' comments, questions, and reactions. The second thing I did was take notes. In this way I trained myself to pay attention and had key sound bites at my ready disposal if I needed to reflect back key points in a discussion. When the meeting ended, I usually shredded the notes, their purpose having been served. Over time, as I became familiar with the most prevalent voices in each meeting, I could almost see the body language through vocal tone, inflection, and cadence. Each voice had its own personality, as did mine.

Persuasion is the second tool worthy of mastery. For some the term persuasion evokes a vision of manipulating or assaulting someone with your opinion until you win them over. Nothing could be further from the truth. Persuasion, done correctly, is built upon honest, respectful, congenial engagement. In his 2001 *Harvard Business Review* article, Robert B. Cialdini, reframing the classical work of Dale Carnegie,[6] outlines the six principles of persuasion.

First is the principle of liking. People like people who like them, so look for things you genuinely admire in others and praise them. The second principle is the principle of reciprocity. People are naturally inclined to repay in kind, so give freely that which you wish to receive. The third principle is that of social proof. The premise here is that people will follow the lead of similar others, so use peer pressure as you are able. Principle four is consistency. People align with clear commitments, so make those commitments active, public, and voluntary. Number five is the principle of authority. People gladly defer to experts, so shine a light on your expertise; don't assume it is self-evident. The sixth and last principle is that of scarcity. People want more of what is rare or not easily available, so highlight unique benefits and exclusive features.

Establishing a strong guiding coalition will guarantee a strong backbone for your EHR governance processes. Guard against the coalition being driven by one or two strong personalities. Use tools (some described here and others that you may have available to you) to grow the group into a team that values equity and a shared vision. Invoke shared decision-making and a desire to actively listen and reach consensus.

Chapter Summary

- A guiding coalition comprised of a minimum number of skilled, credible, influential leaders and managers from across the organization is needed to keep EHR change processes on track and counter organizational resistance.
- Credibility is the foundation of a high-functioning coalition; power is the glue.
- Physician engagement in coalition efforts enables mastery, autonomy, and purpose.
- A guiding coalition should be a team unified in achieving a common goal.
- Physician leadership is *necessary but not sufficient* for EHR governance.
- Respecting others' opinions is a hallmark of a strong guiding coalition.
- Tools like reflective listening and persuasion foster coalition maturity and effectiveness.

Chapter Exercises

It's time to define the members of your guiding coalition and document them in your EHR Governance Toolkit. These can be actual names of people that you know or titles in your organization who would be a key voice with a stake in your EHR governance processes. Aim for diversity and equity with a mix of management and non-management. The members of your guiding coalition should have power, expertise, and be credible. Avoid naysayers, nihilists, and narcissists.

Chapter 6

Create a Vision and a Strategy

> Vision without action is a dream. Action without vision is simply passing the time. Action with vision is making a positive difference.
>
> **– Joel Barker**

Core Values

The vision you create for your EHR governance should be an inspired picture of the future that is appealing to your stakeholders and easy to communicate. This vision typically transcends the data that is used to support official documents such as your IT road map and is more about the overarching direction in which the organization needs to move to create and support strong EHR governance. It is not unusual to have your initial vision crafted by a charismatic leader, well-intentioned but at times slightly out of focus. Don't be afraid to start there and refine your vision iteratively over the first three to six to nine months with input from a variety of perspectives applying a mixture of critical thinking and out-of-the-box brain storming.

According to a 1996 *Harvard Business Review* article by James Collins and Jerry Porras,[1] the two components of any lasting vision are core ideology and an envisioned future. Core ideology defines what something stands for and why it exists. When we think about this in the context of creating an EHR governance structure, it represents an identity or brand that transcends a given change request or project life cycle, new feature or module,

DOI: 10.4324/9781003008408-8

management fad, or individual leader. Core ideology provides the framework that EHR governance processes are built around. It is something that is discovered by looking within at your organization and culture; it cannot be copied or faked. Envisioned future, as the name suggests, is a vision of what your future looks like as a result of your actions. This is more easily defined once you've solidified your core ideology.

Core ideology has two distinct components: (1) purpose and (2) values. Core purpose asks us to answer the question "Why Am I Here?" while core values challenge us to respond to "What Do I Stand For?" These are foundational identity questions for any EHR governance process but also solid level-setting questions for any topic you may be presenting.

Core purpose is the reason EHR governance exists. An effective purpose reflects idealistic motivations for doing the company's work. It doesn't just describe the organization's output or target customers; it captures the soul of the organization. For example, one organization that I worked with had an EHR governance process that was built upon a simple, unvarnished core purpose that resonated well with our leaders and end users – to improve the user experience. They even named the team, *The User Experience Team*, which was in and of itself message branding that was quite effective. And the core values identified in support of user experience allowed both leaders and end users to anticipate and expect a consistent set of behaviors and actions from the team. When challenged by a unique problem that had to be solved in a timely manner, the user experience team routinely fell back on its core values to guide the response.

It is impossible to think of all the possible change requests that can be made in an EHR governance process. One day it's a group of providers threatening a return to paper if they can't have custom order sets built to their specifications. Another day, it's leadership requesting the rapid design and deployment of a smart alert to support the new best practice blood therapeutics workflow. And yet another day, it's your antimicrobial stewardship program pushing for therapeutic substitutions in dozens of order sets to prevent the overuse of designer antibiotics that lead to drug resistance. Each of these requests is a high priority for the person or group making it. The pressure from many different directions can, at times, be stressful. This is where you want to cling desperately to your core values like an old lady clutching her handbag. Seriously, these rules of the road will go a long way in preventing issues like pulling rank, unilateral decision-making, favoritism, and more. Of course, to be effective, all stakeholders in your governance process must agree to support and uphold these values.

The user experience team mentioned above did a great job with this. They defined and embraced six core values for EHR governance processes that were tightly aligned to their purpose (Figure 6.1). The first two, voice and choice, became a rallying cry and signaled clearly and consistently that the heart of the governance structure was the decision body. We will discuss the importance of the decision body in greater detail later in this chapter. For now, it is important to understand that the values of voice and choice established an expectation that physicians and EHR governance shared a joint commitment to improving the user experience which would, in turn, have positive downstream consequences on the physician–patient relationship. Physicians were empowered and expected to exercise the power of their voice to make choices aligned to that goal.

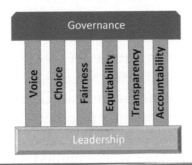

Figure 6.1 **An example of six core values for EHR governance embraced by a large healthcare system.**

The remaining four core values – fairness, equitability, transparency, and accountability –played a supporting but equally important role in defining EHR governance processes. These values were directly linked to the pressing provider problems the user experience team was tasked with solving and provided the momentum required to develop solutions that were driven by explicit, defensible logic and data, not heated passions or quid pro quo.

Fairness is the quality of being marked by impartiality and honesty, free from self-interest, prejudice, or favoritism. This means that everyone is playing by the same governance rules on a level playing field. Who you know doesn't give you an untoward advantage to call in favors or jump ahead in the queue, and leaders are strongly discouraged from using their authority to pull rank. This is intimately linked to the core value of equitability which is dealing equally with all concerned. Transparency is the characteristic of being easy to see through and marks a commitment to eliminating the idea that EHR governance could be a black hole. This empowered the building of tracking tools and dashboards for change requests, so it was easy to see where a request was at any point in time. Accountability is answerability, blameworthiness, liability, and the expectation of account-giving. The user experience team was responsible and accountable for EHR governance processes. Good, bad, or ugly, the buck stopped with them.

With these core values in place, requests for special dispensations decreased and when they did occur, the requestor was more tolerant of having the request declined understanding the impact that their request had on others patiently waiting their turn. However, these situations can place your guiding coalition in a sticky position, so the importance of everyone buying into the same rules of engagement cannot be overstated. Discordance between actions and core values severs trust and credibility which requires a great deal of work to repair.

To be effective you need only a handful of core values. And that makes sense since only a few values can be so deeply held that they will seldom, if ever change. To identify the core values of your EHR governance structure, push with relentless honesty to define what truly matters. If you come up with more than five or six, chances are that you are confusing core values (which do not change) with operating practices, business strategies, or cultural norms (which should be open to change). Remember, the values must stand the test of time. After you've drafted a preliminary list of the core values, ask about each one. A good litmus test question to answer is, if the circumstances changed and *penalized* us for holding this core value, would we still keep it? If you can't honestly answer yes, then the value is not core and should be dropped from consideration.

Governance Framework

At the heart of the user-centric, consensus-driven governance framework is the decision-making body that operates according to parliamentary procedure with no line item vetoes. If you work in a small hospital or practice, a single decision-making body with broad representation may suffice. In a large healthcare system, multiple decision-making bodies with both acute and ambulatory representation will likely be required. Decision-making bodies will need to handle physician-facing requests, nurse-facing requests, and other types of requests like those from the pharmacy or lab. For simplicity in explaining the model, the figures in this book depict three physician decision-making bodies – general acute, general ambulatory, and specialty-specific (Figure 6.2).

Figure 6.2 An example of three different physician decision-making bodies. Many others are possible for other physician specialties, nurses, allied health professionals, etc.

Before a request came to one or more decision-making bodies, it was vetted through a gatekeeper function called routing (Figure 6.3). The routing committee is a cross-disciplinary team with representation from physicians, nursing, pharmacy, ancillary, technical, optimization, build, quality, health information management (HIM), and compliance. Depending on the

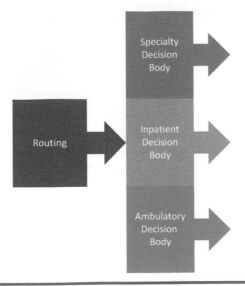

Figure 6.3 The gatekeeper function, routing, reviews all change requests for completeness, technical feasibility, and supporting data. Routing determines what group or groups need to vote upon a given change request.

number of requests being managed, this group may meet every one-to-two weeks. Routing ensures that (1) the change-request ticket submission is complete and technically feasible, (2) there are appropriate analytics in support of the requested change, and (3) the change request is routed expeditiously to the correct decision body for a vote. Routing is the go-to group for most questions regarding change request tickets leading to the (catchy) phrase *when in doubt, route.* As the decision-making body is the heart of EHR governance, routing is the secret to change request throughput and efficiencies.

The resourcing committee, as the name implies, resourced approved change requests for build and release activities. Resourcing applied a First-In-First-Out (FIFO) principle and did not alter the build priority (Figure 6.4). Resourcing essentially put an approved change request on the build conveyer belt.

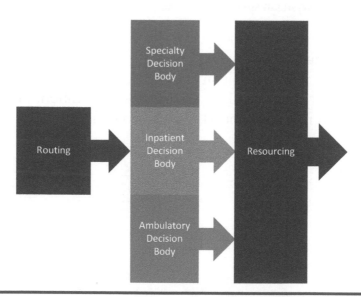

Figure 6.4 Resourcing takes approved change requests and moves them forward for build and release activities.

Once a change request is built, it must still pass through a number of other steps before being released into the live (production) environment (Figure 6.5). This includes validation, testing, release notes, and training. Those activities were tightly cross aligned with EHR governance processes.

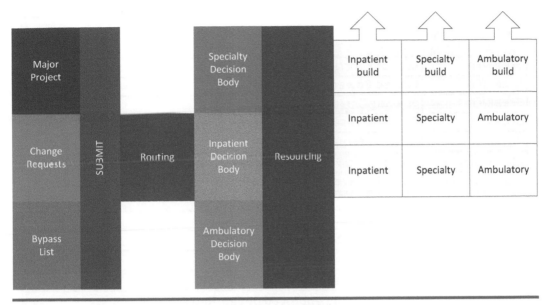

Figure 6.5 **Change requests require validation, testing, release notes, and training before being released into the live EHR environment.**

EHR change requests were submitted to routing from a variety of constituents including clinical informaticists (on behalf of end users), optimization projects, pharmacy, and more. Regardless of the source, every submitted
change request required a complete business case to support it (Chapter 4).
Change requests that were deemed incomplete, not best practice, or mis-
aligned with internal design standards were returned to the requestor for
additional information or evidence. The reason for a change request submission (e.g., event driven response, patient safety concerns, new guidelines,
etc.) was expected to be easily identified within the business case and
appropriate documentation needed to be attached. The routing committee
coordinated with appropriate leadership to vet these requests to promote
safe and high-quality care pathways. If it was determined to not proceed
with a request, the routing committee worked with the change requestor to
develop other technically feasible options that met best practice standards.

Not all change requests are created equal and not all changes made to
the EHR require governance. Some problems are more appropriately and
rapidly addressed with a help desk ticket vetted through a daily change
control meeting. Others can bypass formal governance processes based on
expert mediation, and, finally, there are those change requests that are eligible for automatic bypass. Let's look at some examples that fall into each of
these categories (Figure 6.6).

CATEGORY	CHANGE TYPE
Break/Fix	Loss of Functionality (Worked yesterday and not today)
Break/Fix	Locked PowerNote/DynDoc
Break/Fix	Spelling Corrections
Break/Fix	OEF Field is setup for facility flexing and additional facilties
Break/Fix	Order Reference Text
Maintenance	Synonyms (existing in your domain)
Maintenance	Virtual View on/off (existing orders and plans in your domain)
General	Rules/Alerts (facility Specific)
General	Requisition Routing
General	Scheduling Resources
General	Order Catalog flexing
General	Lab Rad Orders approved by Lab/Rad Council
General	Depart Templates
General	Radiology DCP Synonyms
General	"Other" missing from dropdown
General	Last Charted Value Confirmation
General	"Unable to Obtain" on required fields
General	Charge Issues
General	Domain Sync
General	Minor Report Adjustments

Figure 6.6 Examples of change request types that do *not* benefit from the structured review offered by EHR governance processes.

There are two types of changes that are best handled through a help desk ticket, a break/fix request and most routine maintenance requests. A break/fix is something that worked yesterday but it isn't working today. Examples of breaks/fixes include loss of functionality, spelling corrections, flexing an order entry field for a new site or location, order reference text, and locked documents. Maintenance is routine upkeep and includes, among other things, requests for synonyms or turning an existing order or plan on or off.

Bypass is something sent to governance that is determined not to require decision-body refinement or voting. A governance bypass list is something you will grow over time as you vet requests through your processes. Bypass can be either automatic or mediated by an expert. Examples include build or design errors (if caught quickly this could also be managed through a help desk ticket), discharge templates, an *other* option missing from a drop-down, charge issues, domain syncs (if you have more than one domain), minor report adjustments, last charted value confirmation, etc. A good rule of thumb is that if a change request impacts a provider, it should have their approval and not be bypassed. However, there are situations where a request impacts a provider but is something they cannot vote down (e.g., a regulatory requirement). In these situations, a change might be reviewed and approved for bypass by an expert, or the change might be brought to agenda for design input only (no vote).

To strive for continuity across processes and teams, standardized design templates should be developed for specific types of change request submissions (Table 6.1). This makes it easy for the requestor to know what type of documentation to include with a given type of request and helps guarantee that all the information required for timely build, testing, and release is included in the change request up-front. To improve change request continuity, some type of document versioning should also be observed. For example, change requestors might mark all archived or irrelevant attachments in a request with a *zz* prefix to improve communication between the meeting coordinators and facilitators. This also improves the seamlessness of the decision-making body meetings by having the most relevant and up-to-date content attached to the agendas.

Some organizations seek to iron out all the details of their EHR governance strategy prior to taking the first step. That fully baked process is neither practical nor wise simply because good governance must be fluid

Table 6.1   Standardized Intake Forms Required for Specific Types of Change Request Submissions

Type of Change	Required Form
Rule Alert	Rule Specification Template
Forms	Clinical Document Build Design Template
Orders Order Sets	CPOE Design Form
Reports Smart Template Autotext	Programing Language Specification Form

enough to be responsive to the evolving needs of the constituents it serves. Within agile software development circles, the creation of something with just enough features to satisfy early customers and provide feedback for the future is called the minimum viable product or MVP. If you think of your initial EHR governance strategy as an MVP, then governance design becomes an ongoing, iterative process driven by data and user insights. An EHR governance framework developed in this fashion assures that value is delivered at each step along the way. While this may prove challenging for those not familiar with agile methods, the benefits of crisp, nimble, and responsive governance processes are well worth the learning curve involved.

Decision-Making Bodies

Decision-making bodies are the heart of a user-centric, consensus-driven EHR governance strategy. In this section, we will explore the recommended composition of physician decision-making bodies as well as the roles and responsibilities of key members involved in supporting these groups. A detailed amount of information is provided to allow for easy scaling to non-physician groups and organizations of differing sizes. In a small organization, several of these roles may be performed by a single person, and in a large enterprise system comprised of many entities, there may be several people responsible for each role identified (Figure 6.7).

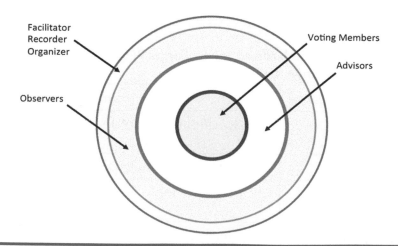

Figure 6.7 **Voting members are the heart of the decision-making body and supported by several key groups including advisors, observers, and meeting support staff.**

Voting Members: Voting members, the core of the decision-making body, are (in the case of physician-facing change requests) actively practicing physicians. If a decision-making body is specialty-specific, the physician must practice within that specialty. Voting members should receive their governance meeting agenda at least one week in advance of the meeting so they have adequate time to consult with colleagues on requested changes to ensure that they represent the voice of their constituency. They then provide feedback and design refinement on the agenda items during the actual meeting. Occasionally, a voting member may also be called upon to participate in an ad hoc design session. A time commitment of approximately two hours per month should be allocated for a voting member to participate in a single EHR governance meeting.

Chairperson: The chairperson is one of the physician voting members of the decision-making body elected to a one-year term. Each decision body should have one chair, but co-chairs may be elected, if needed. If co-chairs are elected there shall be only one chair per meeting, ideally selected beforehand and rotated. The chairperson provides guidance to change request discussions and ensures voting compliance. This person serves as the voice for potential collateral impact and has the authority to require that a request be reviewed by another decision-body group. The chairperson participates in the prep meeting; gives edits or approval of minutes; and monitors the health of EHR governance processes, escalating issues or risks as appropriate. A time commitment of approximately three hours per month should be allocated for a chairperson to lead a single group that meets every month.

Advisory Members: Advisory members are non-voting subject matter experts (SMEs) who participate in discussions on topics related to their area of expertise. SMEs are usually invited into a meeting in support of a specific voting item that is pertinent to them, but some teams such as pharmacy or build may elect to have representation available in every meeting, pre-emptively. While there is a high amount of variability, a time commitment of one to two hours per month should be allocated for SMEs to participate in EHR governance processes.

Observer Members: Decision-body meetings are open to observers who play a role in socializing requests and fostering adoption. Like all other members of the decision-making body, they receive agendas and minutes. Some chairs encourage thoughtful comments from observer members and others request that they participate in listen-mode only. While there is a high amount of variability, a time commitment of one to two hours per month should be allocated for observer members to participate in EHR governance processes.

Facilitator: The facilitator is a neutral, non-voting member with the skillset to prepare and facilitate the decision-making body meeting. This person connects multiple teams, monitors the health of EHR governance processes, and escalates issues or risks, as appropriate. The facilitator may also be called upon to establish and facilitate ad hoc meetings, as required. A time commitment of approximately eight hours per month should be allocated for a facilitator to manage a single group that meets every two weeks.

Recorder: The meeting recorder is a non-voting member who documents decision-making body meeting minutes. A time commitment of approximately three hours per month should be allocated for a meeting recorder to manage a single group that meets every two weeks.

Organizer: The organizer creates the agenda with inputs from the chair, facilitator, and recorder. They coordinate the prep meeting logistics; create and maintain the decision-body membership roster; procure bios for any individual nominated as a chair or co-chair; maintain the organization of meeting documents; create and send decision-body and prep meeting invites; distribute meeting agendas, attachments, and minutes; and determine who will chair if a decision body has co-chairs. A time commitment of approximately ten hours per month should be allocated for an organizer to manage a single group that meets every two weeks.

Clinical Informaticist: The clinical informaticist, or in smaller organizations the clinical person functioning as the bridge between IT and clinicians, is a non-voting member who tracks the change requests that will be included on an agenda; participates in the agenda prep meeting together with the facilitator and decision-body chair; updates the status of a given change request within the defect management software following the meeting; serves as a subject matter expert; and manages action items and follow up activities. A time commitment of approximately eight to ten hours per month should be allocated for a clinical informaticist to engage with a single group that meets every two weeks.

Change Requestor: Every change request brought to agenda has an associated change requestor or ticket owner responsible for presenting the business case, providing the supporting documentation, and refining the proposed solution. The change requestor is responsible for championing the change, building consensus, ensuring the ongoing integrity of the change request, and developing the communication materials required for successful deployment and adoption. A time commitment of approximately six hours per request should be allocated for a change requestor to participate in EHR governance processes.

Decision-making body meetings observe parliamentary procedure. To proceed with a vote, a governance decision-making body must have a minimum of 50% quorum. This requirement can be waived by the chair or co-chairs for the first six months after a new decision-making body group is launched. However, this must be clearly documented by the meeting recorder in both the minutes and change request ticket. After the six-month grace period, the standard quorum requirement of 50% will be reinstated. If the quorum is still not met, the meeting will be canceled, and requests will be pushed to the next agenda.

If quorum is not met, it is crucial for the decision-making body members to crowd source their respective constituents to rally their physician counterparts for the next meeting. However, if these further attempts are unsuccessful and quorum is still not met two consecutive times, the change request will roll up to a broader parent decision-making body for an official vote.

Once roll call indicates that a quorum is present, the facilitator begins the meeting. If any change requests have been tagged as self-evident and placed on a consent agenda, that is where the facilitator will begin. A majority vote is required for a change request to be approved. The facilitator is required to begin the voting process with the voting member most closely aligned to the change request under consideration (e.g., from their facility or region). In the instance that a physician votes to abstain, that vote is not counted in the majority vote.

You may find that well-meaning stakeholders request that an administrator, a nurse practitioner, a midlevel provider, or a medical assistant vote on physician impacting requests in lieu of a physician. If possible, refrain from doing this since it weakens the accountability of any change challenged as a result of a less than perfect outcome. If a physician voting member is occasionally unable to be in attendance, she/he is eligible to nominate a proxy to vote on his/her behalf. A proxy can be either a facility representative or physician representative that the original voting member has nominated to speak on his/her behalf. Prior to nominating a proxy for a decision-making body meeting, the voting member must review the requests in detail and present his voting decision to the nominee (proxy) who will then present an official decision at the meeting. Communication to the facilitator for proxy voting is required prior to meeting commencement. If communication is not received prior to meeting commencement, the authority to approve/deny a proxy for the absent physician is given to the chair/co-chair of the decision-making body.

To respect the time constraints on decision-body meetings, all informational tickets (non-voting) are placed at the bottom of the agenda. If time permits and the change requestor is in attendance, the group can review the informational items and proceed to answer any questions. In the event there is no time left, the informational item may be pushed to the next agenda or at the requestor's discretion be emailed along with the meeting minutes. Likewise, all opt-in tickets (tickets where a specific group must specifically communicate the desire to have a change made) should also be placed at the bottom of the agenda. If time permits, the requestor will be given a maximum of two minutes to share the request utilizing an SBAR (Situation, Background, Assessment, Recommendation) format. It is the responsibility of each voting member to review any opt-in request and socialize it with their respective constituents, as appropriate. If the decision is made to opt in, a representative is required to update the comments section of the change request with this information.

The decision to cancel or reschedule a meeting will be approved by the chair and an explanation of the cancellation will be attached to the meeting cancellation notice which will be distributed at least five days in advance of the scheduled meeting. All attempts should be made to proceed with the scheduled meeting. If a group that meets monthly cancels twice within a five-month period, the cadence of the group should be permanently changed to quarterly, bi-monthly, or pop-up format in deference to the members' schedules.

Design Standards

The EHR design work that accompanies governance can be unwieldy in the absence of design standards. There are two broad categories where clearly defined design standards will be a saving grace. The first is in establishing and maintaining internal consistency within the EHR, and the second is in facilitating external interoperability. For the former, organizations including the Institute for Safe Medical Practices (ISMP) and the HIMSS Electronic Health Record Association (EHRA) recommend several design standards to prevent errors and improve usability. Let's briefly mention a few of many possible examples:

1. *Drug Names with Tall Man Letters*: The ISMP, FDA, Joint Commission (TJC), and other safety-focused organizations have promoted the use of Tall Man (uppercase) letters in the EHR as one means of reducing confusion between similar drug names. Since 2008, the ISMP has maintained a list of drug name pairs and trios with recommended, bolded tall man letters to help draw attention to the dissimilarities in look-alike drug names. Medication names are often provided by a content vendor separate from the EHR developer, meaning that support of this standard is not always within the EHR developer's control. However, EHRs should store medication names in a way that is case-sensitive and can support this guideline.

2. *Standardized Alert Structure*: Use a standard, simple structure for all alerts. This can be achieved by using a relevant and structured approach within each alert: (1) a consistent signal word indicating the seriousness of the alert, (2) information about the hazard (e.g., the drug-drug interaction), (3) instructions or actions to mitigate the hazard, and (4) specific clinical consequences that may ensue if the hazard is not averted. Simplification reduces the effort required for users to visually perceive and interpret critical alerts.

3. *A Single Method for Flagging Abnormalities:* Display numeric and text results clearly. Clinicians must be able to respond correctly to lab results that indicate the presence of a problem. Results that are outside of the range that would be expected for a given patient are particularly important, whether they are outside of a reference range individually or represent an abnormal change from previous results.

4. *Minimize Scrolling*: Keep the information needed to make a clinical judgment on the same page and do not require horizontal scrolling to see critical information. If the screen is not displaying a full message such as a long comment, be sure there is a clear way to see the rest of the message (dragging a scroll bar, clicking an arrow to expand a panel).

5. *Use Commas and Leading Zeros*: Use a comma to separate groups of three digits. A long, continuous string of numbers, particularly if there are many zeros, is hard to interpret correctly. For numbers greater

than 1,000, use the location-appropriate thousands separator. This aids visual interpretation of large numbers by breaking them up into groups of thousands and avoiding misreading errors. Fractional numbers should be displayed with a 0 (zero) before the decimal point. Leading zeros make it less likely that a reader will overlook the decimal point in a fractional number and misinterpret the value. Do not display a trailing zero after the decimal point unless precision is relevant. Including a decimal and trailing zero when displaying a whole number may cause the reader to misinterpret and inflate the value. For example, 1 may be interpreted as 10 if it is expressed with a decimal and trailing zero (1.0).

6. *Differentiate between "No Value Recorded" and "Actually No Value":* Make the difference between *no value recorded* and *actually no value* clear to users. Provide an indicator to inform the user when a result value has not been entered versus when the result is actually a null value. A zero should not be used to represent a null value, since a zero is a value. It is better to use non-numerical identifiers, like dashes (–) or N/A to show that there is no value.

While it is reasonable to consider your EHR vendor standards as the foundation of your internal design standards, you shouldn't adopt everything recommended without cause or question. There are times when you'll want to do something differently for very specific reasons. Take the time to understand the upside and downside associated with a given recommendation and make an informed decision. Alignment with the EHR vendor standard allows you to take full advantage of their product roadmap including the latest features and upgrades as well as the retirement of functions that will no longer be supported. This proved helpful to one organization I worked with as we transitioned from a highly structured documentation process to a workflow-driven, free-text type of documentation process. Hospitals that went live on their EHRs many years ago had been trained on the older (more structured) note type and felt comfortable with it. They were able to easily copy forward parts of their note day-to-day and had often spent considerable time and effort to set up pre-completed templates with macros that allowed them to write a note with a few mouse clicks. While the new workflow-driven documentation process was more intuitive and generated a much nicer looking, easy-to-read note, it required learning a new way of doing things and abandoning the effort that had been expended to adopt and refine the old process. In the end, the EHR vendor announced that the old note type would be retired and that they would not entertain requests for further enhancements or optimizations. This translated into our EHR governance processes mirroring the same process. We no longer accepted change requests for old note types and championed the many benefits of the new workflow that was being adopted as the documentation standard for the organization. This slowly nudged end users toward a new way of doing things.

In addition to the design standards that you adopt within your EHR, you'll want to work with your build team to establish style guidelines for the structured organization of your order sets. For example, the style guideline for all non-ED order sets dictated the following headings be used in this order:

- ADT/Consents
- Vital Signs
- Activity
- Patient Care
- Respiratory
- Diet
- IV Solutions
- Medications
- Laboratory
- Diagnostic Tests (Radiology)
- Consults

This ensured a consistent expectation and experience when using an order set. When a provider was looking for medications within an order set, she/he knew that they could be found after Diet and IV Solutions but before Laboratory. We also collaborated with our build team to develop an annotation standard for mocking up change request documents. New information was highlighted green, information that needed to be removed was highlighted blue, and information that was being changed was highlighted yellow (see Box). Prior to creating this system of green, blue, and yellow highlights, requests would be mocked-up and submitted in many ways. Some requests used track change or strikethrough functions. Some requests used different color fonts. Some requests used before/after screen shots. Some requests used comments, and more. The variability in this process was the underlying cause of significant delays and incomplete build for many a change request.

When making annotations to the Word
version of an order set document, please
observe the following standard:
Green Highlight = Add
Blue Highlight = Remove
Yellow Highlight = Change
Please put any notes and/or comments in a
text box.

The second opportunity to leverage design standards is for interoperability between entities. Herein lies the opportunity to transform a health system from a static, siloed system of care into an integrated learning environment that addresses the continuum of care for the individual, community, and population. With 94% of non-federal acute care hospitals and 78% of office-based physicians using a certified EHR to collect electronic data about patients, the pump appears to be primed for interoperability to become a reality. However, certain complexities still exist.

Today one in three consumers are still burdened with providing their own health information when seeking care for a medical problem. This number is higher if the information needs to cross state lines since most states have different laws and regulations on health information sharing. In addition, the average Medicare patient sees seven providers annually; the typical primary care physician coordinates care with 229 other physicians working in 117 practices; and slightly more than half of all hospitals can electronically search for critical health information from outside sources.

For two systems to be interoperable, they must be able to exchange data and subsequently present that data such that it can be understood. Interoperability happens at four different levels: foundational, structural, semantic, and organizational.

Foundational interoperability is the ability of one IT system to send data to another IT system. The receiving IT system does not necessarily need to be able to interpret the exchanged data – it must simply be able to acknowledge receipt of the data payload. This is the most basic tier of interoperability.

To achieve the second level of interoperability, structural, the recipient system should be able to interpret information at the data field level. This is an intermediate level of interoperability.

Semantic interoperability (level 3) is the ability of health IT systems to exchange and interpret information and then actively use the information that has been exchanged. Semantic interoperability takes advantage of both the structuring of the data exchange and the codification of the data using a vocabulary standard, so the receiving IT systems can interpret the data. Achieving semantic interoperability allows providers to exchange patient summary information with other caregivers and authorized parties using different EHR systems to reduce duplicative testing, enable better-informed clinical decision-making, and avoid adverse health events.

Organizational interoperability refers to ways the healthcare industry, the government, and others are working to provide considerations and standards surrounding interoperability. To this end, on March 9, 2020, the 21st Century Cures Act final rules on interoperability and data blocking were released. On April 5, 2021, the information blocking provisions officially went into effect, setting the expectation that now health data should be instantaneously available as long as it's electronic. This much-anticipated legislation marked a milestone in the ongoing pursuit of consumer access to personal health data and the removal of barriers to meaningful information-sharing. It also defined the conditions for certification that would be used to achieve this vision.

For example, the rule promotes common standards through the United States Core Data for Interoperability (USCDI). USCDI, the new name for CCDS (Common Clinical Data Set), defined the standardized set of health data classes and data elements (which now includes provenance) that are essential for nationwide, interoperable health information exchange. The USCDI includes medications, allergies, clinical notes, and other clinical data to help improve the exchange of electronic health information and ensures that the information can be effectively understood when it is received. The standards also include demographic data to support accurate patient identification across care settings.

While there are a variety of relevant healthcare standards for connecting labs, images, claims processing, and more, the Cures Act mandates HL7® FHIR® (Fast Healthcare Interoperability Resources)[2] Release 4 as the secure, internet-based data standard application programming interface (API) requirement to support patient access and control of their electronic health information. The HL7® FHIR® Release 4 standard defines how healthcare information can be exchanged between different computer systems regardless of how it is stored in those systems. It allows healthcare information, including clinical and administrative data, to be available securely to those who have a need to access it and to those who have the right to do so for the benefit of a patient receiving care. By adopting existing standards and technologies already familiar to software developers, FHIR significantly lowers the barriers of entry for new software developers to support healthcare needs.

Since FHIR was originally launched, it has been used by healthcare application implementers across the globe, including the payer community, drawn by its ease of use. This has led to a large online community supported by web-accessible specifications, community-developed tooling, servers, and libraries. FHIR is also utilized by other healthcare standards organizations such as IHE (Integrating the Healthcare Enterprise 4). While the information requirements of healthcare data are extremely complex, the HL7® FHIR® standard is a landmark step to remove many of the barriers to healthcare data exchange.

While enthusiasm for FHIR is high, the health IT standard is not without its drawbacks. EHR vendors have placed restrictions on the use of FHIR, making them read-only. There is understandable skepticism about importing outside clinical data into the EHR without validation. This prevents any app powered by FHIR from triggering a workflow within the EHR. This limits the usefulness of FHIR and will impede its adoption.

Chapter Summary

- A vision is an inspired picture of the future that is appealing to stakeholders and easy to communicate.
- Your core purpose defines *what* your processes stand for and your core values are *why* your processes exist.
- You will have no more than five to six core values and they do not change over time.
- Providing a high-level strategic framework will support your EHR governance vision.
- Decision bodies are the heart of EHR governance.
- Routing and resourcing are teams that help optimize the movement of change requests through governance processes.
- A few well-defined roles and responsibilities are needed to seamlessly support user-centric, consensus-driven EHR governance processes.
- Parliamentary procedure, as classically outlined in Roberts Rules of Order, is the organizational framework for EHR governance voting meetings. These may be amended early on, for a limited time, to reflect the special needs of a newly forming group.
- Design standards are useful in maintaining internal consistency and external interoperability.
- The Institute for Safe Medical Practices (ISMP) and the HIMSS Electronic Health Record Association (EHRA) recommend several design standards to prevent errors and improve usability.
- The future of interoperability standards changed on March 9, 2020, with the adoption of the 21st Century Cures Act final rules and again on April 5, 2021, with the deployment of information blocking regulations.
- United States Core Data for Interoperability (USCDI) defined the standardized set of health data classes and data elements (which now includes provenance) that are essential for nationwide, interoperable health information exchange.
- HL7® FHIR® (Fast Healthcare Interoperability Resources) Release 4 was mandated as the secure, internet-based data standard application programming interface (API) requirement to support patient access and control of their electronic health information.

Chapter Exercises

1. Now it is time to *discover* your core ideology. You do not deduce it by looking at the external environment. You understand it by looking inside. Ideology has to be authentic. You cannot fake it. You should have no more than five to six core values. Litmus test your list by asking, *if the circumstances changed and penalized us for holding this core value, would we still keep it?* If you can't honestly answer yes, then the value is not core and should be dropped from consideration. Add this information to your EHR Governance Toolkit.

2. In this chapter, we mapped one possible strategic framework for EHR governance processes. You will now do the same. Feel free to borrow, refine, or start from scratch. It's important that you start with a minimum viable product (the essentials) knowing that after you launch your governance processes, you will expand and continuously refine your framework. Add this information to your EHR Governance Toolkit.

3. The process and procedure for standing up your EHR governance voting groups and running your governance meetings will be one of the largest sections of your EHR Governance Toolkit. Using classic parliamentary procedure as your foundation, feel free to address EHR governance-specific roles and responsibilities. Also include special needs that you may have early on as voting members are being identified and groups are forming. Add this information to your EHR Governance Toolkit.

4. Identify the design standards you want to adopt for your EHR governance processes. Consider starting with your EHR vendor's standards and refining from there. Add this information to your EHR Governance Toolkit.

Chapter 7

Communicate the Vision

If you have an important point to make, don't try to be subtle or clever. Use a pile driver. Hit the point once. Then come back and hit it again. Then hit it a third time – a tremendous whack.

– Winston Churchill

Assumptions Are the Termites of Communication

Now that you've drafted a vision and strategy for your EHR governance, you'll want to share it broadly and get buy-in. Herein lies a great challenge simply because most people operate under the assumption that if they communicate something, those on the receiving end of their message have learned something. This is a dangerous assumption and, more times than not, incorrect.

I worked with a senior executive at a large healthcare system who was fond of town hall meetings for sharing information and obtaining feedback. These events were professionally organized and moderated with in-person and virtual attendance options. There were often several hundred attendees at these meetings which sounds like a good turn out until you realize that the organization employed over 62,000 people. Another senior executive engaged resources to develop a MailChimp distribution list with over 13,000 emails so that brief, compelling emails could be sent directly to a specific target audience of professionals, when necessary. That sounds more impactful until you look at the metrics which reported that only a fraction of the

DOI: 10.4324/9781003008408-9

target audience clicked on the actual email and a fraction of that fraction actually read the message. Yet another approach was a phone app that was a communication, education, and defect reporting tool. The product was slick but the target physician audience was hesitant to load yet one more app on their phone without proof of its usefulness. They proved difficult to convince and uptake was slow. Over time, as the product and its value matured, I imagine the uptake would have reached a tipping point where peer-to-peer engagement and pressure caused it to go viral. Unfortunately we'll never know because the app product support was discontinued as a result of a change in leadership and digital priorities. Other communication methods include newsletters, flyers, pamphlets, educational tools, and videos. In short, there is no lack of tools for sharing information. And that's a good thing because getting information into the hands of busy professionals is hard; and then assuming that this constitutes communicating is, at best, hopeful.

The first rule of communication is that there is no such thing as overcommunication. Do it early, do it often. Communication is not a one-and-done deal. Remember, different people like to be communicated with in different ways so utilize different types of tools and both synchronous and asynchronous delivery methods. Do it in small groups, in large groups, one-on-one. Some specific suggestions worth considering:

1. Use your internal communication channels to spread the word. The old vidal sassoon commercial made this concept of a communication cascade famous; you tell a friend and they tell a friend, and so on, and so on. Only in this case, you build rapport and credibility by directly communicating with your peers and direct reports and they then do the same with their peers and direct reports and so on. When doing this, it is best to provide standardized content or talking points that can be easily shared so the messaging remains crisp and doesn't suffer from reframing or modification. If possible, conduct a stakeholder review to help you identify the various groups you need to communicate with. Understanding how each stakeholder group will be impacted by your initiative will help you target the messaging based on what will be most important, interesting and relevant for each group to know.

2. Explain why. People find it easier to accept a change when they understand why that change is being made. You have plenty of material from the earlier chapters in this book to craft a clear and compelling answer to this question. Just be sure to keep it simple and focused.

Long-winded and detailed explanations will lose all but the most interested audience members (and they aren't the difficult ones to reach).

3. Provide context. Just as the first section of this book provided you with context regarding a user-centric, consensus-driven model for EHR governance, so too should your communication provide context regarding your vision. This allows your audience to integrate and align your message with the mission or roadmap of the larger organization.

4. Tell stories and avoid jargon. Maya Angelou famously said, *people will forget what you said, people will forget what you did, but people will never forget how you made them feel.* Frame your vision with stories and examples that people can relate to. Healthcare is about serving people and, in the end, EHR governance is about serving the end user so they can serve their patients.

5. Use innovation. A short video that is well done can be a powerful tool. If a picture is worth 1,000 words, what's a video worth? Facebook, Twitter, and Instagram – social media tools tap into a group of people that are difficult to reach any other way. If your company uses an internal communication tool like Slack or Ryver, consider a message in select group forums. As digital innovation continues to explode, be creative with how you leverage it to get your message out.

6. Stay humble and true to your core values. This falls into the category of actions speak louder than words, or more accurately, when your actions and your words are not aligned, people believe your actions and you lose credibility. For example, if one of your core values is accountability and you place the blame elsewhere for an issue related to your EHR governance processes, people will be less likely to trust what you say. Never hesitate to say *I don't know* when you don't know something. It may make you feel vulnerable or uncomfortable at the time, but if you evade the issue or make something up that is later found not to be true, your trust equity may take a hit.

Communication Skills and Traditions

Once you've committed to a strong communication strategy (congratulations), it's time to hone specific skills that can successfully communicate your EHR governance processes. In her book *The Power of Presence*, Kristi Hedges points to five specific interaction types that should be mastered: (1) creating an intentional presence, (2) being able to get buy-in, (3) delivering executive briefings, (4) connecting with distributed teams through digital resources, and (5) giving and receiving direct feedback.[1]

Not that long ago, the prevailing way most organizations got work done was through hierarchy. Your boss told you what to do, you told your direct reports what to do and so on, and so on, down the line. However, in an era marked by rapid growth and innovation, this command-and-control style of leadership has fallen into disfavor as organizations recognize its stifling impact upon agility and transformation. As teams become more multidisciplinary in composition and their hierarchical structures flatten, work now gets done through influence and personal presence. For some, perhaps the term personal presence evokes the idea of a polished, smooth-talking salesman. But that's not the spirit of personal presence at all, even though a person with personal presence is often polished and persuasive. Personal presence is the ability to connect with and inspire others. It is, above all other things, genuine, and if faked will not succeed. It reflects a self-awareness that allows you to be comfortable with who you are and mindful of how your thoughts and actions interact with each other and impact others. *What do I want my presence to convey? How do I want to make people feel?* One of the best ways to learn personal presence is to observe someone who has it. Drill down to the specifics and consider what you might need to change if you wanted to be perceived the same way.

For your EHR governance processes to be successful you'll need support. But buy-in isn't always so easy to come by. In the past, it was often obtained by successfully presenting and defending your fully baked proposal to a steering committee or leadership team that was empowered to approve or deny it. This describe-and-defend model left little if any room to socialize ideas and get input from other resources including the experts conducting the review. Today the model is shifting to a paradigm where the idea is presented while still in the development phase. This is done purposefully to let others help create the plan and allow for early and iterative communication. Dialing in other resources early on leads to stronger proposals with greater buy-in from the start.

Providing a succinct and engaging executive briefing is a bread-and-butter communication skill that the EHR governance team leaders should be comfortable with. In many organizations, this skill earns you a seat at the table. The key, of course, is to get to the point – quickly. To do this, your presentation starts with your takeaway message. What's your sound bite, your conclusion, your bottom line? Next frame the *why*. Slides should be uncluttered, visually pleasing, and easy to read. This means using concise bullet points instead of sentences or paragraphs. Specificity adds value and the target audience should be the most senior person in the room. Leave adequate time for questions and answers. Responses should not be evasive, argumentative, or oppositional but rather should evoke a sense of enthusiasm. Practice answering difficult questions with a colleague until you feel comfortable with pivoting, using the room, or co-opting an argument successfully.

Virtual teams in matrixed organizations are becoming more common, requiring greater communication, not less. It is not unusual for these teams to utilize a variety of communication tools including email, virtual meetings, instant messaging, a communication platform, and a storage tool. This is in addition to their normal social media venues. The energy being put into virtual presence and branding is huge and at times, bigger than life. So how do we take advantage of this for our EHR governance processes? First, remember the need for human interaction. If possible, have a 15-minute daily huddle with your team each morning. Expect that all people join the meeting with their video on and the format be straightforward and engaging. For example, I used to huddle with my informatics team once a week using a template that covered five areas:

1. Information for the Week (awareness for the rest of the team)
2. Recognition/Team Achievements (make someone's day)
3. Obstacles/Improvements (challenges and actions to take)
4. Organizational Updates (things impacting our team)
5. Initiative Updates (successes, challenges, awareness)

Hosting and recording responsibilities rotated on a weekly basis and minutes were posted into a folder on our Microsoft Teams site for easy access. Also remember to take full advantage of your virtual presence. When you give a presentation, turn on your video. Don't hide behind your presentation. Don't read from a script or be robotic. Do ask for participation. Be mindful of the lack of body language or cues and articulate the unspoken. Simply put, do everything you can to humanize the virtual engagement and interaction.

The last of our five interactions, giving and receiving feedback, is a skill that people either embrace or run away from. Those who embrace feedback assume positive intent and consider it a growth opportunity. Those who recoil from feedback often feel they are being criticized and misunderstood.

For feedback to be effective, it should be as close to real time as possible and provide context. Anecdotal feedback provided days to months afterwards is challenging to digest and act upon. A tip that Ms. Hedges shares when offering feedback is to intentionally frame what you say by focusing on your intended reaction. That is simply ask yourself how you want the person to react in response to your feedback. Perhaps you want them to take it seriously while remaining reassured that you have their back. What should you say to evoke that feeling?

This section would be incomplete without briefly touching upon SBARs and Visio diagrams. These are communication methods often used to convey problems and workflow issues within the EHR. SBARs are the mainstay of nursing communication, although they are used widely outside of nursing, as well. The situation (S) provides a brief, succinct overview of what the issue is. Background (B) states the pertinent history and tells us what got us to the current state. Assessment (A) summarizes the facts and gives you an idea of what is going on. Recommendation (R) states what you are looking for and suggests what needs to happen next. Utilizing an SBAR format in EHR governance may make it easier for clinicians to organize their thoughts and present a clearer business case for a change request.

Visio diagrams are usually the tool of choice for conveying workflows (Figure 7.1). Swim lanes are created for each group that has a role in each process and actions are mapped between the swim lanes with great specificity.

Somewhere in the human genome there is a gene that, when expressed, allows people to communicate fluently using Visio diagrams; I don't believe many physicians have it. I've seen some of the finest providers I know get glassy-eyed when a project manager with good intentions walks them, step-by-step, through a series of diamonds and circles connected by lines or arrows pointing up, down, and sideways. It's often painful, and the goal of communicating with the provider might be better served by succinct bullet points in a slide presentation.

There is one place in EHR governance where Visio diagrams are the communication tool of choice. That is mapping the explicit logic required for a clinical decision support (CDS) request. Here, the detail afforded by a Visio creates a bridge between the design team and the build team, ensuring all the moving pieces of the CDS request are captured appropriately and tested accurately.

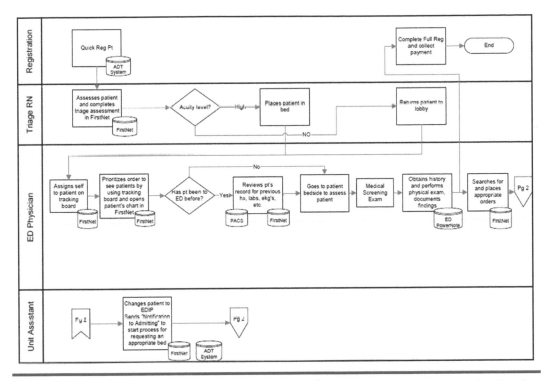

Figure 7.1 **A typical Visio diagram conveying a detailed process using standardized symbols across multiple groups depicted by different swim lanes.**

Who Told You That?

Have you ever wondered why one person can share a message and it catches on fire and that exact same message shared by another person falls flat? In this section we are going to discuss the messenger, not the message, because without a trusted communicator many hearts and minds are never captured.

Research shows that decision-makers will often place their faith less in what is being said, and more in who is saying it. Following a trusted authority often reduces feelings of uncertainty which is invaluable in today's constantly changing business environment. So how do you convince your audience that you have the credibility to make a recommendation that they can feel good about? Most effective messengers have three key attributes: expertise, trustworthiness, and similarity.

Expertise is knowledge in a particular area. When people feel uncertain, they typically look to experts to guide their decisions. You need to be seen as competent and knowledgeable, yet recounting a list of your accomplishments, successes, and triumphs, however impressive, will do little to endear you to others. No one likes a braggart. But arranging for someone to do it on your behalf can be a remarkably efficient tactic in overcoming the self-promotion dilemma. Take, for example, a set of studies led by Stanford University's Jeffrey Pfeffer,[2] who found that arranging for an intermediary to toot your horn can be very effective. Participants in one study were asked to play the role of a book publisher dealing with an experienced and successful author and read excerpts from a negotiation for a sizable book advance. Half read excerpts from the agent, touting the author's accomplishments. The other group read identical comments made by the author himself. The results were clear. Participants rated the author much more favorably on nearly every dimension – especially likeability – when the author's agent sang his praises instead of the author himself. Remarkably, despite the fact that participants were aware that agents have a financial interest in their authors' success and were therefore biased, hardly any took this into account.

In another study with real estate agents, researchers measured the impact of a receptionist introducing a realtor's credentials before putting through a call from a prospective client. Customers interested in selling a property were truthfully informed of the agent's qualifications and training before the inquiry was routed to them. The impact of this honest and cost-free introduction was impressive. The agency immediately measured a 19.6% rise in the number of appointments they booked compared to when no introductions were made. So arranging for others to tout your expertise before you make your case can increase the likelihood of people paying attention and acting on your advice.

Brain scans showed that in the presence of expert advice, the area of the brain linked to critical thinking and counter-arguing flat-lined. This is discordant with the traditional assumption that people listen to advice, integrate it with their own information, and then come to a decision. If that were true, activity in the brain region that guides decisions would have been seen. However, when people received expert advice, that processing activity went away. So, if you can claim relevant expertise make that clear, in a subtle manner, early on. For those who already do a good job of telegraphing their expertise, the following two points will also be important.

Trustworthiness is the quality of being believable. In ambiguous, uncertain, or controversial situations where multiple answers vie for credibility, it can be tempting for a messenger to conceal any small doubts or uncertainties about their message by sweeping them under the carpet, believing they could be detrimental to success. However, evidence suggests that signaling small uncertainties or doubts immediately before the delivery of the strongest argument actually has valuable trust-raising qualities. Sequencing is the key lesson here. Start your message with a small weakness or drawback, then use the word *but* before delivering your strongest message. A doctor who says, *No vaccine in the world is without the occasional adverse event, but this vaccine is extremely safe and has been used to protect millions of children,* strengthens her trustworthiness and credibility. But notice how your reaction to the message feels different if the weakness follows, rather than precedes, the strength.

Similarity is the quality of resembling another. We're more likely to believe people who are like us. This notion is the basis of peer group engagements such as smoking cessation groups or weight loss programs. And that makes sense. Imagine a middle-aged woman comes to you because she wants to stop smoking. She began smoking in high school to fit in with her circle of friends and figured she could quit whenever she wanted to. She managed to cut back to just a few cigarettes per day during her two pregnancies but immediately resumed after delivering her children. Today she smokes two packs per day and is frustrated by how expensive it is and with her children telling her that she smells like cigarette smoke all the time. As her physician, you have both the expertise and the trustworthiness to give her tools and tips for smoking cessation. You might suggest chewing gum, drinking water, and exercising more while using a medication to reduce the cravings and withdrawal symptoms. This is a time-honored approach to getting the job done but you, as the messenger, lack the credibility that gets infused into the message when it comes from someone who has known, firsthand, the struggles of nicotine withdrawal. That same advice from someone who smoked two packs of cigarettes per day for 12 years and kicked the habit successfully is much more likely to lead to results. The lesson here is that even though you may be the best qualified person to deliver your message, you may not be the most effective messenger. There are times when having someone else deliver the message will achieve the best results.

Communication comes in both word and deed. Nothing undermines change more than behavior by important individuals that is inconsistent with their verbal communication, and nothing is more powerful than the alignment between the two. Take Elon Musk, the founder of Tesla electric cars, for example. In 2014, he made more than 100 patents effectively open source:

> Tesla Motors was created to accelerate the advent of sustainable transport. If we clear a path to the creation of compelling electric vehicles, but then lay intellectual property landmines behind us to inhibit others, we are acting in a manner contrary to that goal. Tesla will not initiate patent lawsuits against anyone who, in good faith, wants to use our technology.[3]

Normally patents are used to keep other companies from using proprietary knowledge for their own benefit because that could hurt the innovator's income. However, Musk's strategy was to make it easier for other manufacturers to get into the electric vehicle (EV) market, not harder. More companies making more EVs will increase the demand for charging stations to be set up around the country and world. And other companies will finance much of that infrastructure. More infrastructure will increase demand for EVs. This is a very strategic move and well-aligned to Musk's objective of reducing the number of internal combustion engines on the road and the pollution they cause.

Chapter Summary

■ Communicating something on your end doesn't necessarily translate into something being learned by the person on the receiving end.

■ You cannot overcommunicate your vision. Take advantage of tools that allow you to:
  - Use your internal communication channels.
  - Explain why.
  - Provide context.
  - Tell stories and avoid jargon.
  - Use innovation.
  - Stay humble and true to your core values.

■ There are specific skills that will assist with communicating effectively:
  - Creating an intentional presence
  - Being able to get buy-in
  - Delivering executive briefings
  - Connecting with distributed teams through digital resources
  - Giving and receiving direct feedback
  - SBARs and Visios

■ Using a trusted communicator to share your EHR governance vision conveys expertise, trustworthiness, and similarity.

■ What you communicate and how you behave must be in alignment. Discordance between words and actions will engender mistrust.

Chapter Exercises

For the communication section of your EHR Governance Toolkit, you'll want to capture the variety of ways you'll communicate your vision to different stakeholder groups.

1. Who are the existing communication resources in your organization? This person or team of people are often happy to convey information through well-established routes and share standardized tools and templates that will make communications easier.
2. How can you partner with your Medical Staff Office (MSO) and Chief Medical Officer (CMO)? The MSO maintains a database of physician contact information (including personal cell and email information) that originates from credentialing. They are protective of this information and partner with the CMO to determine what types of communications they will send to physicians.
3. What other communication resources can you leverage?
    a. Existing newsletters
    b. Social media
    c. Communication platforms (e.g., Slack, Ryver)
    d. Video loop in the physician lounge
    e. Cascading word-of-mouth
    f. Team retreats
    g. Medical staff meetings
    h. Medical Executive Committee (MEC) meetings
    i. Executive briefings
    j. A standing agenda item in your own governance meetings
    k. Daily huddles
4. The person delivering a communication (who) is just as important, if not more important, as what is being communicated. The ideal attributes of the communicator were discussed in the chapter (expertise, trustworthiness, and similarity). Ideally this should be a physician leader highly engaged, visible, and accountable in EHR governance processes.

Chapter 8

Remove Obstacles

If you can find a path with no obstacles, it probably doesn't lead anywhere.

– Frank A. Clark

The Allure of Inertia

The number one obstacle to change is inertia. The term *inertia* comes from the Latin root for *inert,* which means lacking the ability to move. The law of inertia, also known as Newton's first law of motion, states that an object at rest stays at rest and an object in motion stays in motion with the same speed and in the same direction unless acted upon by an unbalanced force. This simple law of physics helps us to understand why once someone has settled into a routine, it is no simple matter to change that process, *even if the change represents a better process.* This is an energy-sparing response in a species hard-wired to use energy conservatively. This tendency to prefer that one's environment and situation remain as they already are is known as status quo bias. Status quo bias is most impactful in the realm of decision-making, meaning that when we make decisions, we tend to prefer the more familiar choice over the less familiar one. This inclination toward the path of least resistance is the very reason that doing nothing is appealing.

Inertia on a large scale can signal that you don't have broad-enough buy-in for your efforts or that there is change fatigue. Consider this scenario, which will be familiar to most if not all of you. A well-intentioned leader enthusiastically pitches an innovative initiative that will move the needle on a major problem. Her town hall presentation seems to be just the right blend of information and inspiration to ignite passion. The room buzzes and there is a feeling, at least at that moment, of broad buy-in. But once the lights go down and the crowd disperses, the chatter begins. People dig their heels in and make comments like *I'll wait this one out*; *I'll pass*; *It's just another fad*. These types of comments from the rare few who are always naysayers are par for the course. However, if you are hearing this from a larger swath of your constituency or key influencers, beware. Pay attention to the warning signs.

Like most of you, I'm inclined toward doing things a certain way. As a physician I've spent many years honing a skill and a skillset. I've been shaped by many a noble tradition in medicine as well as a deep and abiding passion for data and evidence-based practice. When I had my own office, I had a specific way of doing things. I surrounded myself with other practitioners, support staff, and extenders to create a culture that anchored my expertise and offered my patients the best possible care I could give. For the most part, I was not looking to have my workflow disrupted on a regular basis and was skeptical of too much change too quickly. Yet outside of the office, I had an alter ego. At home I was a paragon of home improvement change – knocking down walls, building garden structures, refinishing floors, installing new lighting. I loved to watch the home and garden television shows for new ideas and then try them out. I was fearless and bold. Much to my husband's chagrin and eventual delight, change was constant.

So, what's the difference between these two versions of me? Well, in my professional life, change was being pushed at me from the outside – insurance companies, payers, medical conferences, licensing requirements, professional accreditation standards, medical malpractice, and more. My mastery and autonomy as a physician were under constant siege with the possibility that unintended consequences could have a downstream impact on a patient or my staff. In my personal life, change was self-initiated. I decided on the project. I picked the tools, the materials, and the timing. I was the master of my project and its destiny. If it went well, good for me. If it required professional assistance and resuscitation, well, that was okay too. Unanticipated problems were easily corrected, and no one was any the worse for the learning experience.

So how do we overcome the impact that inertia can have on EHR governance adoption and acceptance? While every organization is different and every situation warrants its own approach, these three tips are worth considering to help break free of the status quo. First, work with key influencers. If you are lucky, several of these people are already part of your guiding coalition. If not, you'll need to take the time to get buy-in from them. These are the colleagues that physicians look to for advice; the go-to people to discuss a case or problem solve. They usually offer you the credibility, support, and influence that you need to move forward.

Next, be transparent about the bad and the ugly. That is, explicitly make the cost of poor reliability or failure clear to the teams engaged in your governance processes. Share the data, share the complaints, the quality concerns, and the safety concerns. Share all of it so people feel empowered to go the extra mile to make a difference.

Finally, celebrate successes. This can't be done too often and must be genuine. When your team gathers, always spend a few minutes on recognitions and team achievements. It was the rare day when there was nothing called out for this. Perhaps a person facilitated a difficult meeting with great finesse the day before or the target adoption goal for beta testing was achieved or a new feature was released or someone passed their project management exam. The point is, share these stories every day as moments of triumph and reflect upon how they have an impact on your mission.

Breaking free of organizational inertia may be one of the greatest achievements on your EHR governance journey. A certain amount of momentum is required to break free of the status quo but consistency and ongoing vigilance is required to stay free until a new way of doing things takes hold. Falling back into old habits and routines will be the path of least resistance for some time, so it is important to help people envision themselves in a better future.

Change is the Only Constant in Life

One of the 16 lessons that branding guru Scott Bedbury (think the Nike *Just Do It* campaign) shares from a lifetime in marketing is, just because you can wear spandex doesn't mean that you should. Likewise, in EHR governance, the question that we ask ourselves on a regular basis is, *Just because you can change something, does it mean you should?* In an idyllic environment filled with change agents who have access to unlimited resources, perhaps the answer to that question is yes. In the real world, however, there is always a need to identify the rate-limiting step or steps in how much change an EHR governance framework can effectively process and how much end users will tolerate.

In Chapter 4, we walked through the change request lifecycle. Let's briefly summarize the series of successive steps that need to happen in a particular order to produce the desired change in the EHR. The first step entails translating the problem into a complete and technically feasible change request. This request must then move through the appropriate decision body or decision bodies for review, refinement, and sign-off. Next, it's onto the resourcing conveyor belt where it is built and tested. Communication is attached and socialized and voila, it is released. While this is a high-level view of a much more nuanced process, it is useful in helping to identify major bottlenecks at transition points that require attention. Are too many requests coming in at the beginning and getting backed up there? Are decision bodies overwhelmed with the number of items moving to their agendas? Are the build queues backed up with wait times that exceed service level agreement expectations? Or perhaps the communication team is having difficulty maintaining traction with socializing new functionality?

The answers to these questions are best driven by data on throughput, TAT, and specific time-motion metrics. In one organization, when we first stood up our new governance processes, we purposely opened the flood gate, placing no restriction on the number of requests that could be submitted. We were confident the new framework could handle a much larger number of requests with a much quicker TAT, and we were eager to show our end users that this was not business as usual with a coat of paint to make it look pretty.

Within 18 months, throughput increased four-fold and TAT was cut by more than 50%. As we studied the data, we saw the largest number of requests were coming from three of the eight regions comprising the organization, with the other five not being nearly as active. To encourage equity, we capped the number of requests that could be submitted by any particular region. Our resourcing and communication teams also reported some backlog in their queues, so we moved to a more frequent release cycle. We learned that you can't solve the problem you don't know about; you can't remove the obstacle you don't see. Our teams communicated by email, instant messaging, and on a communication platform daily. We had a formal one-hour meeting every other week and did a more formal in-person session every six weeks or so. We were constantly monitoring key data and problem-solving to address obstacles and prevent small issues from growing into large ones.

Change tolerance was another issue that we monitored closely. When the new framework was stood up, the complaint from our end users was that change was too slow. We weren't exactly sure what too much change looked like, but we were listening for warning signs of change saturation. This needed to be carefully balanced against the business leader's *more-is-better* mindset. Change fatigue, if not recognized and addressed, often leads to withdrawal and disengagement from processes. But how do you know when someone is fatigued?

Research indicates that people have differing opinions on how much change is too much and that the answer, much like the perception of beauty, may be in the eye of the beholder. This became evident when we sent an EHR user experience survey to our providers and asked them: *What was the most significant improvement you have seen (in the EHR) in the past 12 months?* A colleague created a word cloud to reflect the answers received (Figure 8.1). We were intrigued by the large number of *nones* and wondered if that meant the respondent didn't know about the changes that were made, didn't embrace the changes that were made, or perhaps were part of a specialty group that truly had a small amount of change. As we explored further, we were amazed by what appeared to be a dueling dynamic in some of the comments. Negative comments included: *The system is even more difficult to use as order sets and templates are 'upgraded' and the templates are horrid. Poor workflow is the worst part. Click boxes not easy to make.*

Figure 8.1   A word cloud of the responses from physicians in a large healthcare system to the question: *What was the most significant improvement you have seen (in the EHR) in the past 12 months?*

While providers reporting a positive experience commented: *Frequent updates to order sets; Some order sets have been tailored to the needs of clinical end-users; Orders actually work now and go to the right locations; Easy use of templates; and Personalized templates.* Same EHR platform, same amount of change being deployed across the system, yet one group of physicians had positive things to say while the other group was somewhat indifferent or disgruntled. This same phenomenon was reported by KLAS analytics in a worldwide study done in different organizations on different EHR platforms.

As uncomfortable as change can be, it isn't going away. In fact, most healthcare organizations anticipate needing to be able to manage more change with fewer resources in the coming years. This means people may be less tolerant of change and experience change fatigue behaviors like disengagement, apathy, indifference, burnout, stress, anxiety, confusion, complaining, cynicism, and more. However, a few tricks applied proactively may help ease this burden.

Use the work done in the past as a foundation for creating the future. Team members want to know that their prior efforts weren't a waste of time. If they feel criticized or dismissed, gaining buy-in for a new vision will be hard, if not impossible.

Everyone who has caught the Lean bug likes to *go to the gemba*, that is, to go out, listen, show respect, and collect feedback. And that makes sense because who better than the worker knows the work? Who better than the end user knows the EHR?

Commit to a culture of continuous improvement. EHR governance is not a one-and-done undertaking, so make a point of never treating it as such.

Identify clear objectives and the key metrics you will track for meeting them. Leading with the data is a great way to level set on team progress and work effort.

Take pride in failing and failing quickly. To come up with great ideas, failures are inevitable. If you aren't failing on a regular basis, you aren't innovating.

Resistance is Futile

In the scheme of obstacles to EHR governance processes, resisters are the group that use their energy to actively push back. The people in this group have a wide variety of personalities, although some of the most effective resisters I've ever encountered have been clever, articulate, snarky, and charismatic. They may have been labeled as problem makers, naysayers, or backbiters, and that was usually a point of pride on their parts. They often held positions with some authority and their colleagues revered them as the voice of reason. Base Commander Colonel Nathan Jessup, Jack Nicholson's character, in *A Few Good Men*, is a perfect fictional example.

Personally, I love resisters for two reasons – they engage and they are the first to notice the faults. Resisters become a great value to EHR governance processes if you can successfully channel their energy for the greater good. The key to working effectively with a resister is to tease apart the constructive from the destructive and respond with transparency and accountability.

One of my more memorable experiences with a resister was when a member of my team invited me to join her for a *Health Check* being done for one of our family medicine residency programs. A *Health Check*, in our governance parlance, was a rapid cycle process improvement opportunity aimed at aligning user interface and workflows with best practice standards. My teammate shared that while prepping for the visit, several people commented that they were trained to do something a specific way that was contrary to the current standard. Curious to know more and finding our *Health Checks* a great learning experience, I happily tagged along. On the second day of the visit, the person who was training the residents showed up to give an ad hoc training session. The residents were thrilled and clearly had the highest regard for this person. Arriving a few minutes late to the session, I slipped in at the back of the room. As soon as I had adjusted myself comfortably in the chair, I was called out for the specific things that EHR governance did that were onerous and unproductive. Honestly, some of the points made were well-taken, but others were not. I marveled at the confidence exuded by this trainer, even when misquoting several facts and figures. I willed myself not to push back or become defensive. I quietly took notes and corrected one or two overt mistakes. Afterwards, my teammate and I debriefed by grouping the information shared into three columns: places where the trainer and the standard agreed, places where the trainer and the standard disagreed but there were no downstream consequences and places where the trainer and the standard disagreed and there were potential downstream consequences. We agreed to focus only on correcting the third column.

As I was driving home, I called the trainer and shared the results of the debriefing. I also inquired about the source of the data shared since it wasn't consistent with the facts and figures I had. We exchanged emails over the next few days until, in one email, the trainer confessed that he felt like he was getting his hand slapped. I conveyed the great respect I had for him but that I was dispassionate about the data and simply wanted to make sure that the residency program was well situated for any audit or review it might be engaged in. As we talked further, he confessed that he was a self-proclaimed, hot-blooded Latino who was very passionate about everything and that my approach felt cold and unfriendly to him. We laughed together at our shared realization and tied up the remaining loose ends on the *Health Check*. In the end we agreed on more things than we disagreed on.

When it comes to resisters, Sun Tzu, a famed Chinese general and military strategist, and Michael Corleone, the main protagonist of Mario Puzo's novel *The Godfather*, offer the same advice:[1] keep your friends close and your enemies closer. Actually, Sun Tzu is being paraphrased here since the quote in *The Art of War* is:

> If you know the enemy and know yourself, you need not fear the result of a hundred battles. If you know yourself but not the enemy, for every victory gained you will also suffer a defeat. If you know neither the enemy nor yourself, you will succumb in every battle.

Regardless of whether you think of resisters as the enemy (so to speak) or not, embracing them as a valued asset makes great sense for several reasons. First, resisters are the first to notice problems – like the canary who signals toxic gas levels in the coal mine. They recognize potential pain points in the EHR before they mushroom into larger, unwieldy problems. Second, resisters are usually key influencers with a wide circle of impact. Collaborating with a resister may allow your credibility to penetrate groups of people that would otherwise be out of reach. Finally, resisters tend to be energetic and resilient. These two traits will work against your EHR governance processes and keep you up at night if the resister does not buy into what you are doing. However, those same skills focused on optimizing EHR governance are invaluable. These are the people that will chair a decision-body group, beta-test a new functionality, and drive consensus with colleagues. The one caveat, and it's an important one, is that their time be used efficiently and that they see tangible results. In summary, if you see the opportunity to engage with a resister, don't pass it up. Some of the worst critics have the potential to become some of the best champions.

Confusion over Decision Rights

One final obstacle worthy of discussion is clarity regarding decision rights. If your EHR governance processes don't clearly indicate who is responsible for what decisions, people will eventually grow confused and a futile tug-of-war between departments or team members may ensue. Fundamentally, decision-making is a trade-off between the amount of time it takes to make a decision and the level of buy-in that it generates. A quickly made decision by a leader usually has poor buy-in from a large number of stakeholders. Likewise, decisions based upon broad consensus usually take much more time to make.

Early on, when your governance processes are in their formative stages, this may not be a problem. Consensus may entail a few key stakeholders who are easily convened on a regular basis, giving you the ability to have both speed and consensus. However, as your governance matures and the number of stakeholders invested in your processes grows, so too must the clarity of your decision-making methods. Decision rights must be assigned thoughtfully and communicated clearly to ensure role clarity.

Begin by determining the level at which different types of decisions should be made. Decisions made at the enterprise or corporate level should be reserved for issues that impact the company at large. For example, decisions about EHR code upgrades or priorities for your IT road map are best made at the highest leadership level. Decisions primarily impacting the division, region, department, or business unit should be made at that level. And decisions with a primary impact on the employee or team should be made at the local or individual level. No matter the level of decision-making, it is always important to consider the need for cross-functional input to ensure effective coordination. Decision execution is often, if not always, a team sport.

Transparency about decision-making and decision rights needs to be approached in two ways. First, every group should have a meeting cadence that establishes a predictable rhythm for the business. For example, in one organization I worked with, the governance team met the second and fourth Friday of the month for a one-hour meeting and had two, half-day governance design sessions every six weeks. Specialty decision bodies met once a month at a specific day/time for one hour, while the larger umbrella decision bodies met twice a month at a designated date/time for one to two hours. All decision-body meetings were open to anyone who wanted to listen in; however, only physician voting members could cast a vote. All meetings were published in a governance calendar that was open for all to see.

Meeting agendas and minutes were posted to each group on a shared site where they could be easily accessed for review. This ensured that everyone understood what decisions were being made when and by whom.

Second, there is a need to connect and coordinate governing groups that should collaborate on specific decisions. For example, one organization I worked with had a Blood Therapeutics Clinical Council tasked with determining best practice for items related to clinical standards, diagnostic evaluations, therapeutic interventions, medical devices, and new technologies. As part of their mission, this group endorsed a new standard for ordering blood transfusions and recommended a change to the associated workflow. To effectively operationalize this new standard required (among other things) coordinating physician and nursing decision-body groups to review and refine the design, reassessing the lab workflow, making sure the order flowed correctly to the blood bank system, checking associated pharmacy responsibilities, retiring an old order set and deploying a new customized build, and communicating a cutover strategy. Each group had a predictable set of information flowing into their meeting and a defined set of decisions and conclusions coming out, all of which needed to be coordinated to seamlessly deploy this new standard. Determining who can and should make what decisions and how that information gets coordinated in a timely fashion ensures organizational alignment.

With the power to make decisions comes the responsibility to be accountable for them. Herein lies the importance of tracking key performance indicators and feedback. Data-informed decision-making and post-decision analyses are key to how decision rights are updated and decision authority is distributed. Overcentralizing decision-making is an error many organizations fall prey to. Leaders feel pressed for time and are convinced that they can make a better call. But decision rights must be collocated facilitating buy-in and ownership. The secret is including enough key stakeholders to get the job done without grinding the decision-making process to a complete standstill.

Decision rights must be assigned unequivocally. Ambiguity here is probably the greatest obstacle to EHR governance growth and success. It leads either to infighting or paralysis. Either is unacceptable and completely preventable with role clarity.

Finally, always remember that good decisions can, on occasion, result in poor outcomes. Don't reflexively make changes to decision rights without fully understanding the reason for a poor outcome or you may make the matter worse. Role clarity in any organization is controversial and political; one part art, two parts science.

Chapter Summary

- Inertia is the #1 obstacle to EHR governance change. Even if something better is offered, people are often inclined to stick with what they have. This is known as status quo bias and it can be reduced by:
  - Engaging key influencers,
  - Making the cost of failure clear, and
  - Celebrating successes.
- Just because you can change something doesn't mean you should. Key considerations include resource limitations and the tolerance level end users have for embracing too much change.
- Mitigate change fatigue by using past work as a foundation for future work; observing and engaging with frontline workers; being data-driven and focusing on continuous improvement; and giving yourself permission to fail but fail quickly.
- Resisters can be great assets to EHR governance processes because they engage and are the first to notice the faults.
- Lack of clarity over EHR governance roles and responsibilities can quickly derail processes.

Chapter Exercises

1. It's time to identify key proponents of the status quo within your organization. These are often people who have been with the company long enough to see different change initiatives come and go. They aren't usually naysayers but rather have a keen perspective of culture over the long horizon and see themselves as stabilizers in the organization. They require a healthy dose of information, education, and data regarding EHR governance processes, and key leaders with this leaning are ideal candidates for your guiding coalition (Chapter 4). Go ahead and write down the names of those people who fall into this category.

2. Tracking data from the start will allow you to validate your EHR governance processes to your constituents and leaders. Begin with process metrics that have realistic targets. Where will you begin? Turnaround time? Throughput? Time-motion data? Something else? Then slowly move toward capturing outcome data.

3. What person, persons, or group are empowered to make what decisions? Does anyone have veto power? Should anyone? This is part of the parliamentary procedure that you added in Chapter 6, but more. Take the time now to add detail to this area, knowing that you will refine decision rights in real time as use cases emerge.

Chapter 9

Generate Short-Term Wins

The successful person never loses … they either win or learn!

– John Calipari

One Size Doesn't Fit All

Be mindful of the need to engage in impactful change quickly by looking for audacious projects with broad reach. In one large healthcare organization that I worked with, providers were consistently complaining that their EHR user interface was clunky and disruptive. It was difficult to find results and document information. Physicians, regardless of specialty, all saw the same view. This meant that the pediatrician and the surgeon, who had vastly different workflows, both navigated the EHR from a single generic screen. As a result, more and more physician time was spent clicking through the various menus and check boxes required to accomplish even simple tasks. In response, a pilot was conducted with 11 Hospital Medicine physicians and 8 Emergency Medicine physicians across 4 hospitals that moved them out of their current one-size-fits-all generic screen into their own specialty-specific (Hospital Medicine or Emergency Medicine) views (Figure 9.1).

We further asked them to adopt a workflow-driven form of documentation that complemented the specialty interface instead of clicking through the existing structured documentation templates. The new functionality tested in this pilot was the standard build recommended by our EHR vendor, refined with input from the appropriate specialty-physician governance

DOI: 10.4324/9781003008408-11

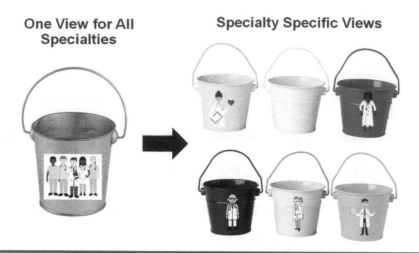

Figure 9.1   **Moving from one user interface for all physicians using the EHR to specialty-specific user interfaces improved user experience in a large healthcare organization.**

bodies. The pilot physicians were supported in their transition by four clinical informaticists (one from each participating hospital).

The pilot was two weeks long. Quantitative baseline metrics were run for the month before the pilot and then again after the pilot ended. Written, web-based modules and virtual training were conducted, and at-the-elbow support was provided for the first ten days. After the formal part of the pilot was concluded, providers were asked for their specific feedback on new functionality and their overall experience with the pilot. Here's what we learned:

- Our 11 Hospital Medicine pilot physicians were able to identify 57 issues, which included major ones such as system slowness and note template functionality.
- Our 8 ED pilot physicians identified 37 issues, including multiple changes to their tracking board view.
- In 2 short weeks, these 19 providers wrote 855 workflow-driven notes providing test functionality and workflow optimization at a very detailed level. This facilitated changes and recommendations that benefited all users going forward.
- All 19 pilot physicians requested the ability to keep the new interface and documentation functionality.
- The integrated testing of downstream interfaces (e.g., HIE, HIM, reports) posed the greatest technical obstacles to operationalizing these new functions.

A post-pilot survey was sent to all the physician participants; 12 of the 19 (63%) responded. Seventy five percent said that the specialty-specific position was more intuitive than the old position; 58% said it was more efficient. All physicians felt the new format for documentation was crisp and easier to read; 40% said it saved them time and 40% liked how it aligned well with workflow. One provider commented, *I am hesitant to embrace the changes (because change is difficult), but condensing down the options and creating good workflow is what this is all about ... And is a good thing.*

Armed with the data, findings, and feedback from this pilot, we partnered with several other groups to develop an organizational strategy to deploy more than 40 specialty-specific positions in a 14-month period (Figure 9.2). As an added benefit, the early adopter physicians who participated in the pilot provided peer support and knowledge for their colleagues.

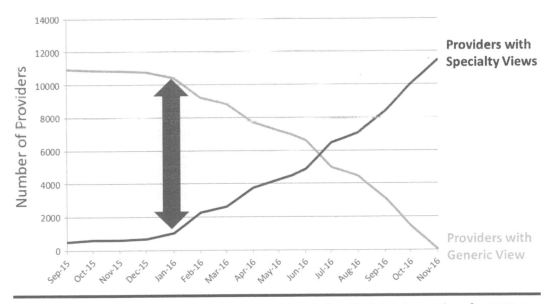

Figure 9.2 **The transition from one user interface for all physicians using the EHR to specialty-specific user interfaces in a large healthcare system over a 14-month period.**

This early win for our governance team, on such a high-visibility project, cemented our credibility as agents of change committed to improving the user's experience with the EHR. This was further reinforced as the team took on other projects, large and small, with the same focus, tenacity, and perseverance. However, trust is a hard thing to win and an easy thing to lose. It represents a fragile balance between respecting who people are, balancing the give and take of relationships, and is founded on the belief that a trusted person will not do something that undermines trust. So, the team was ever vigilant, in everything we did, to advocate for the end user in a fair, equitable, transparent, and accountable manner.

The Pain of Documentation

EHRs made documentation onerous and unfriendly. The earliest versions of the more popular health records were designed to capture discrete fields of information to satisfy the data incentives required to qualify for meaningful use dollars. Physicians found themselves engaged in a never-ending game of point and click within long, poorly customized documentation templates. The notes returned were long and cryptic. The patient's story was lost in translation, and anyone reading the note was challenged to find the key clinical information that used to be face-up in the paper world.

To ease the pain, vendors provided tools that allowed notes to be saved with individualized customization and copied. Savvy providers achieved similar pain relief by dictating into free text fields or creating macros that could be cut and pasted into their EHR documentation. Auditors recognized this phenomenon citing multiple examples of documentation that looked the same from day to day. Some of the more obvious cases highlighted in the Recovery Audit Contract (RAC) audits conducted between 2003 and 2007 showed information unique to a single day copied forward into several subsequent notes. RAC audits recovered over $693 million on behalf of the Centers for Medicare & Medicaid Services (CMS).

The burden electronic documentation placed upon clinicians was acknowledged and perhaps justified too quickly as something that would be mitigated over time, as muscle memory made EHR workflows second nature and technological advances such as natural language processing made it easier to extract key information from free text. There was a prevailing belief that the added value in capturing information that would facilitate safer, high-quality care outweighed the downside of the few minutes of clinician time required to make it happen. And if safer, high-quality care had indeed been the outcome, that perhaps would have been true. However, physicians saw little, if any, upside to the added work they were being asked to perform. In fact, the unintended consequences of digitizing healthcare mounted.[1]

Acutely aware of these issues and their impact upon our providers, one team I worked with partnered in several efforts aimed at lightening the burden of electronic documentation. This included exploring the cost–benefit of using scribes, voice-to-text software, Google Glass™ technology, and a next-generation workflow-driven documentation standard offered by the EHR vendor. It made sense to us that one size would not fit all, so we targeted the groups with the highest level of perceived pain and remained flexible about mixing and matching. For example, our ED physicians had two distinct camps when it came to documentation. The first camp swore by scribes. They lobbied actively on the need for these extenders so they could document efficiently and practice at the top of their license. The ED practice group supported this and was intimately involved with our education team in creating and training to a scribe standard. The second camp of ED physicians argued that scribes slowed them down and were committed to voice-to-text technology tools such as those offered by Nuance or M*Modal. They created short cuts, macros, and templates. They enabled their smartphones as microphones while commandeering multiple workstations to optimize a workflow that hinged upon seeing multiple patients concurrently. The data collected by this group on this approach to documentation became the basis of a compelling business case to purchase an enterprise-wide voice-to-text software license.

As a result of this multi-factorial approach to improving documentation, our standard evolved and became more user friendly. Today, most of those providers use a workflow-driven process to create their documentation which is a better use of time and, anecdotally, more effective at conveying key clinical information to colleagues while maintaining the patient's story. Some specialty groups are still inclined to use a workflow enabled by scribes; however, the organization did eventually purchase an enterprise license for voice-to-text software and developed training to assist with adoption and optimization. Google Glass™ remains a well-utilized tool among innovators in the ambulatory space. As they continually evolve what the clinic of the future will look like, perhaps new ambient voice recognition tools will shift the documentation paradigm once again.

The quest for better documentation is an ongoing journey. It is a significant challenge to penetrate and socialize new functionalities with all end users. In general, our experience has been consistent with what the Gartner hype cycle suggests.[2] New functionality often triggers a peak of inflated expectations followed by a descent into the trough of disillusionment where expectations are reset allowing the journey up the slope of enlightenment to the plateau of broader adoption and productivity (Figure 9.3).

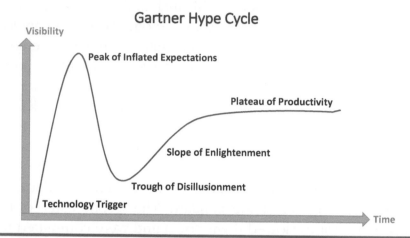

Figure 9.3   New functionality within the EHR often triggers a peak of inflated expectations followed by a descent into the trough of disillusionment where expectations are reset allowing the journey up the slope of enlightenment to the plateau of broader adoption and productivity. Source: Adapted from Gartner Research *(www.gartner.com)*.

For example, an EHR analyst contacted me regarding a root cause analysis she was conducting of a breakdown in our Health Information Exchange (HIE) interface. A physician's progress note that was 37 pages long had crashed our interface capabilities. A review of the content of this note indicated that much of the information was pulled into the document automatically, including all lab results over a long period of time and several full radiology reports. It wasn't clear why the physician wanted that much information in a progress note or if he was aware of just how long the final progress note was. Many other progress notes written by this same physician were also long, although not long enough to break the HIE interface and trigger detection. When this physician and I spoke, it became clear that he was resigned to an EHR interface that was poor and wasn't paying attention to the final length of his notes. He rightfully blamed the EHR for making it hard to do the right thing. Empathizing with the pain and indifference this physician was feeling, yet keenly aware of the downstream impact of these notes on colleagues and the medical record, I persuaded the physician to commit to working with one of the clinical informaticists for no more than one hour to clean up his preferences and templates. The problem did not reoccur, and I like to believe that the physician benefited from the engagement, although I am not sure he would say that.

Tell a Story with the Data

If a tree falls in the forest and no one is around to hear it, does it make a sound? Likewise, if your EHR governance processes generate early wins and no one is aware of them, did they happen? Data is a good communication tool. Stories are a better communication tool. Stories informed and supported by data are an unbeatable communication tool. Using data early on to tell stories about the changes produced as a result of your EHR governance processes is a must.

For example, change request throughput and TAT have been high-profile problems in every organization that I have worked in. It was not unusual to have end users complain quite loudly about how long it took to get a change made in the EHR. Even seemingly simple requests were at times reported to take more than a year to operationalize. Committed to addressing these issues in short order, one team I worked with did a deep dive and came up with a multifaceted approach to tackle the matter. First, the change request process was standardized as described in Chapters 4 and 6. To recap, the intake template was redesigned to require a robust business case, estimates of impact, affected users, build design documents, and designated testers. Then a gatekeeper function was created. This cross-disciplinary team comprised of clinical, technical, compliance, and build experts met on a weekly basis to review all change request submissions for completeness and technical feasibility. This ensured that each request was routed to the correct decision body or decision bodies based upon end user impact, for vetting and vote. The third part of this approach was focused on rebuilding trust and credibility with end users. To do this, the structure and cadence of the largest governance decision bodies were overhauled to be a more efficient and effective use of provider time. Detailed agendas with supporting documentation were shared a week in advance of any given meeting for socialization, feedback, and discussion. And finally, tools were developed to provide transparency into EHR governance processes. A mobile app was created that, much like a UPS tracking system, allowed a user to quickly see where a change request was in its lifecycle. In addition, a self-serve dashboard provided a retrospective snapshot of key EHR governance performance indicators.

Within a year, change request throughput increased more than four-fold with over 300 changes being released into our live EHR environment each quarter in 2015 (Figure 9.4). The TAT for a change request, measured from when it was first submitted to the gatekeeper group to when it was released

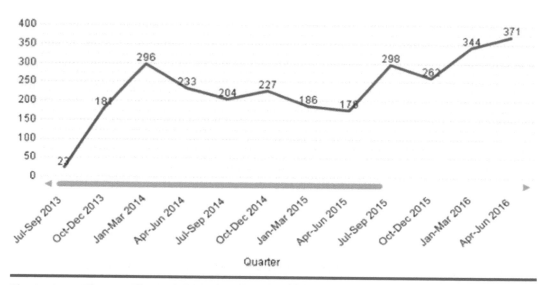

Figure 9.4 **The number of change request tickets that went from being approved to released, by quarter, all tickets in a large healthcare organization, 9/17/13–12/31/16.**

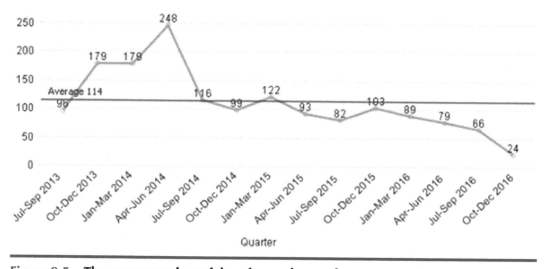

Figure 9.5 **The mean number of days from when a change request was approved until it was closed, by quarter, for all tickets in a large healthcare organization, 9/17/13–12/31/16.**

into the live environment, was slashed by more than half (Figure 9.5). This data was shared with as many stakeholders in as many venues as possible. It was presented in leadership meetings; it was presented as governance updates during decision-body meetings; it was presented to national audiences in well-respected meetings.

As you might imagine, these early wins went a long way in establishing the team's trustworthiness and credibility. We developed the reputation for keeping our promises, cutting through the red tape, and getting the job done. Providers quickly learned that our #1 job was to improve their EHR user experience and that their comments and feedback were taken seriously.

While streamlining process measures early on is a key win, it is important to remain responsive and innovative; not to rest on your laurels. Earlier in this chapter we discussed several other initiatives that were undertaken to meet our end users' needs while simultaneously maturing our governance processes to solidify our reputation. We were ever mindful that trust is hard won and easily lost, so we were vigilant about committing to championing a culture of transparency and accountability (as you recall, two of our core values). This is where John Doerr's book *Measure What Matters* became an invaluable resource.[3]

Doerr introduces us to the world of objectives and key results (OKRs), a management methodology that originated at Intel and spread to industry innovators like Google, LinkedIn, and Zynga. In short, *objectives* tell you where to go and *key results* tell you whether you are going there. Objectives should be ambitious, qualitative and inspirational, strategically aligned, time bound, and provide clear direction. Key results make the objectives achievable; they are measurable, quantifiable, difficult but not impossible, and actionable. Key results are not a task or to-do. Putting a man on the moon is an objective. Launching a lunar module weighing under 40,000 pounds by December 1965 is a key result. At first blush creating OKRs sounds easy to do, but it is surprisingly challenging.

As part of a governance design session, I facilitated a white boarding session with a cross-disciplinary team to develop objectives for EHR governance. Here's what we came up with:

1. Get to *zero defects* for what goes into production.
2. Align the holistic EHR governance process and requests to support the organization's business and clinical goals. This will decrease the volume of change requests being processed while improving the value.
3. Increase the understanding of EHR governance and benefits that come from governance processes. Leverage data captured in training sessions for this.
4. Improve the quality of the design work being done to reduce the burden of the EHR on the end user.
5. Improve the standardization and adoption of the EHR.
6. Ensure that data and best practice inform all decision-making.

After the session, the objectives were socialized with key leaders and sponsors. The feedback was positive, so two other people and I met to draft one to two proposed key results for each objective. We challenged ourselves to clearly identify the data that would inform the numerator and denominator for each key result developed. These couldn't be theoretical, pie-in-the-sky metrics. Some key results were easy to craft while others were painstaking. Overall, the process wasn't as easy as I thought it would be.

One leader, tongue in cheek, was fond of saying, *first the data pisses you off, then it sets you free* – and he was right! Even less-than-wonderful data almost always has a pearl or two within it somewhere if you take the time to understand it and give it context. A few guiding principles help make this process easier. First, determine a single source of truth. There is nothing more frustrating than having different forms of the same data lead to different conclusions. Where appropriate, data should be clean and normalized. There should be a standard approach to handling outliers and imputing missing data. Second, when you are standing up governance processes, take a moment to define how you want to capture the data you want to report on. Will a free text field work or do you need a structured dropdown list of options? Are start and end dates clear and easily extracted? Finally, pick an approach and stick with it. Objectives and key results are not something that we did early on, but knowing what I know today, I wish we had.

Chapter Summary

- Early wins are key to establishing credibility and getting your EHR governance processes off to a good start.
- Prioritize projects that have broad impact and high visibility. The examples discussed in this chapter were strong wins:
  - Specialty-specific user interfaces
  - Workflow-driven documentation
  - Voice-to-text software
- The adoption of new functionality usually unfolds as predicted by the Gartner Hype Cycle:
  - Peak of inflated expectations
  - Descent into the trough of disillusionment where expectations are reset
  - Journey up the slope of enlightenment
  - Plateau of broader adoption and productivity
- A strong and memorable way to communicate your wins is through stories informed by data.
- Consider developing objectives and key results (OKRs), a management methodology that tells you where to go and whether you are going there.
  - Objectives should be ambitious, qualitative and inspirational, strategically aligned, time bound, and provide clear direction.
  - Key results make the objective achievable; they are measurable, quantifiable, difficult but not impossible and actionable.

Chapter Exercises

1. What project or projects can you do early on to establish the credibility and responsiveness of your EHR governance processes? Make a list of projects that have broad impact and respond to the needs of your various EHR constituents.
2. Define the metrics that you want to capture for each project as part of the initial planning process. Envision, when the project is successful, how the metric will be used to frame a story of success.

Chapter 10

Consolidate Gains and Produce More Wins

The only way to win is to learn faster than anyone else.

– Unknown

If you are standing up a new EHR governance process, it will be a year or two until you think about this step of consolidating gains and producing more wins. If you are refining an existing process, you probably have opportunities you can take advantage of now. In this chapter, we will explore three things that teams I worked with did that might inspire you. As you'll see, each opportunity organically presented itself out of an ongoing commitment to iterative improvement cycles and tracking process, time motion, and outcome metrics.

Automate

Automation streamlines processes that are rule-based, structured, and repetitive, thereby freeing up people to focus on more value-adding business activities. As you mature and expand your EHR governance processes you'll identify many opportunities where automation will make you more effective and efficient. For example, in one organization, the meeting coordinators wanted to find a way to automate the back-end busy work that went into extracting a change request from the defect management system to build an agenda. It took two hours for each larger meeting and an hour for each smaller meeting to do this, adding up to almost 20 hours of tedious, rote work per month.

The meeting coordinators met with the data analyst who listened to and observed the manual process used to build meeting agendas. She then

DOI: 10.4324/9781003008408-12

scripted a program that mapped specific fields of information in the defect management system directly into an Excel spreadsheet template. The first tab in the spread sheet listed the titles of all the change request tickets for a specific governance-body agenda. Each ticket then had its own individual tab within the Excel spreadsheet with supporting details and documentation. This was easily reached by a hyperlink from the listing in the first tab.

The logic used to map this process was completely dependent upon accurate structured data in the defect management system as that information was simply mapped from point A (in the defect management system) to point B (in the Excel agenda template). If the defect management system had erroneous information, the agenda had erroneous information. This automated agenda was reviewed in the prep-meeting to refine the change request language and remove any unnecessary information.

Before using the automated agenda with our governance groups for the first time, we gave a demonstration showing how it would work and championed how it was bringing greater efficiencies to our EHR governance processes. The first two times that we sent out an automated agenda for any meeting we also sent a version in the old format to anticipate any problems meeting members might have with the transition. By the third meeting, only the automated agenda was sent. The transition went off without a hitch.

Another place where automation was applied with great success was a process that leveraged data to improve adoption. This shift toward data-driven workflows and platform optimization began with localized site visits that, informed by time, motion, and use metrics, focused on rapid cycle improvement. As the quality of data available matured, so too did the process. Standardized reports were developed that took the individual metrics and aggregated them into a single score reflecting how the provider was doing with their EHR adoption and optimization. Because this score was generated in a standardized automated fashion, it could be generated quickly and used to benchmark progress or decline over time. The development and use of this automated scoring report marked a significant evolution in the program.

Scale

Once your EHR governance processes are humming along (relatively) smoothly, it's time to start thinking about expanding the scope of your work. This will often happen with little prompting as your team develops a reputation for being highly collaborative and getting the job done. Two examples where we did this with constituents who naturally dovetailed with EHR governance processes were clinical decision support (CDS) and pharmacy.

The CDS group was tasked with developing, updating, and maintaining clinically appropriate and relevant rules aimed at improving patient care, safety, and quality outcomes. This group was responsible for design only and all requests coming to them for input required initial sponsorship and final sign-off by an appropriate governance voting body. As you can see from the workflow depicted in Figure 10.1, the CDS process leveraged the existing EHR governance processes outlined in Chapter 6, to design, pilot, and deploy smart processes that made it easier for providers to do the right thing.

As the CDS group developed its charter, guidelines were established:

- Design must begin with a measurable clinical question, business goal, or problem that needs to be solved.
- A design intervention should be based on root cause investigation, as appropriate.
- Prior to an intervention being designed, consideration should be given to what can be done in the workflow to intervene sooner.
- The five rights of CDS must be explicitly applied to each intervention designed (Figure 10.2).[1]
- CDS design should make it easy to do the right thing and hard to do the wrong thing within the clinical workflow and the EHR.
- Baseline metrics for each CDS intervention designed should be evidence-based.
- Post implementation metrics of success should be measured and tracked over time.
- CDS interventions should be linked to improved clinical outcomes.
- CDS interventions should focus on the user experience.
- CDS design may be considered in response to requests for artificial intelligence.
- The unintended consequences of CDS design should be explicitly considered for all interventions.
- Items out of scope included CDS interventions *exclusively* impacting areas with their own separate module (pathology, radiology, and pharmacy).

All CDS alerts required baseline data as part of the initial change request and once deployed, were tracked in an interactive dashboard to validate their value (Figures 10.3–10.5).

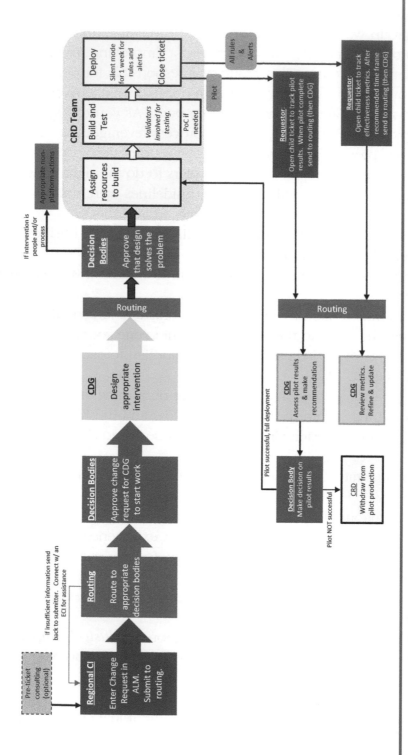

Figure 10.1 **The workflow process for developing clinical decision support (CDS) requests for the EHR in a large healthcare organization.**

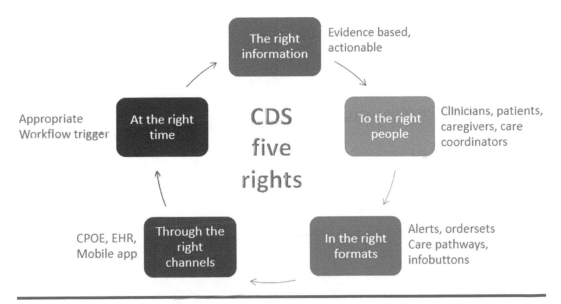

Figure 10.2   The five rights of clinical decision support (CDS) depicted in a circular, iterative fashion. Source: Adapted from the book *Improving Medication Use and Outcome with CDS: A Step-by-Step Guide by* Jerome Osheroff, 2009.

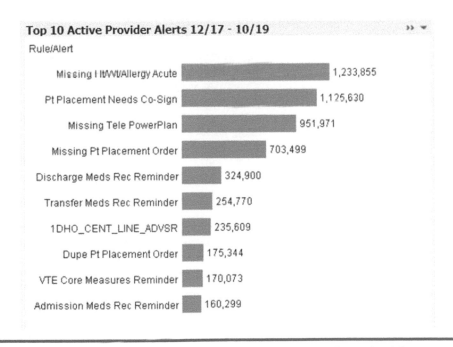

Figure 10.3   The top 10 active provider alerts triggered in a large healthcare organization.

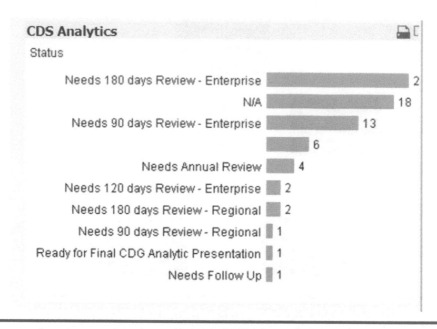

Figure 10.4 The alert analytics in a large healthcare organization.

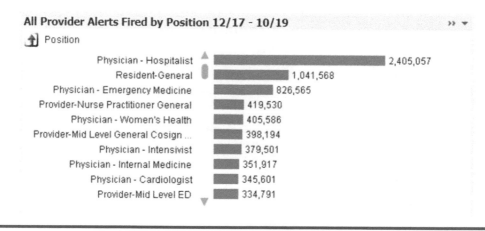

Figure 10.5 The alerts fired by specialty in a large healthcare organization.

Pharmacy was the second team where a mutually beneficial partnership evolved. In the spring of 2017, pharmacy leaders in one organization I worked with invited several EHR governance leaders into a planning session focused on the logistics of creating a standardized formulary across the organization to reduce variation in medication use. This mandate, no small task, had support at the highest level with data supporting an opportunity for safer, high-quality care with significant cost-savings for the organization.

To do this, a pharmacy leadership team, with physician and pharmacy representation from across the organization, was empowered to approve medication practice and formulary work based on clinical data and research recommendations. These best practice recommendations would be made by a medication advisory committee comprised of clinicians and subject matter experts. A pharmacy council was tasked primarily with supply chain issues (e.g., shortages) and finally, the pharmacy informatics design group was responsible for developing the change requests that would be submitted into the traditional EHR governance processes through the gatekeeper group (routing). Routing also had the ability to send requests with medication impact to any of the pharmacy groups, as appropriate. How this was all woven together within the context of existing EHR governance processes is shown in Figure 10.6.

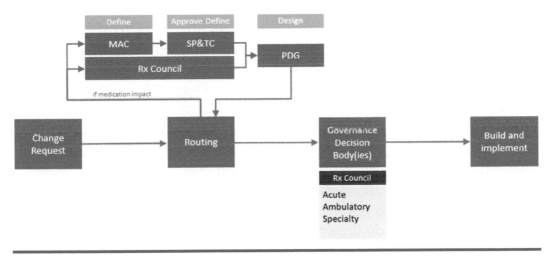

Figure 10.6 The high level process designed for EHR governance to collaborate with pharmacy in standardizing the formulary across a large healthcare organization.

It took several months of joint team efforts to iron out the details involved in this process. For example, the routing group needed criteria to guide and standardize when it was appropriate to send a change request from another source to the pharmacy teams for best practice review and consultation. There was a need for a cut-over strategy to map existing pharmacy-related requests into the governance change request queue. Members of the new pharmacy informatics group needed to be identified, provisioned and trained on how to place change request tickets within the governance change management system, and more.

On September 6, 2017, pharmacy processes formally transitioned into EHR governance processes. The joint team was vigilant in meeting regularly to review data and feedback on what was working well and what wasn't. For example, one thing we hadn't mapped in our initial work was how pharmacy changes would be deployed and communicated. We quickly learned that the processes traditionally used by EHR governance didn't provide enough lead time to socialize pharmacy changes, some of which had far-reaching impact, nor did they touch all the appropriate target audiences consistently. That part of the pharmacy process was redesigned.

It was several months before our issues list organically lightened and the cadence of our joint meetings slowed. However, our commitment to actively refining and improving never waned. On our one-year anniversary we laughed at what we had learned and how far we had come. As I look back now, it's clear that EHR governance was incredibly fortunate to have such highly engaged and motivated partners in pharmacy. This collaboration set the *just right* tone for the other groups that followed. This was helpful when partners couldn't or wouldn't allocate resources or insisted on creating governance shortcuts intended to reduce TAT at the expense of poor processes.

It is the nature of every organization, rightly so, to drive time- and cost-effective processes. However, it is critical to recognize the difference between improved efficiencies and taking short cuts. When you see what looks like the latter, a culture that encourages and respects speaking up is invaluable. All too often poor planning forces emergent action. But if you don't have the time to do it right, when will you have the time to do it over?

Virtual Governance

In one organization that I worked with, there was a core group of physician end users who would engage in optimizing the EHR as long as it did not interfere with their clinical responsibilities, it remained an effective and efficient use of their time, resulted in a better user experience and improved patient care. Despite that commitment, several specialty-specific physician groups were unable to meet quorum month-over-month due to scheduling conflicts, high patient loads, or emergent procedures. In response, an idea was piloted to leverage a virtual asynchronous communication platform (e.g., Slack, Ryver) for physician governance.

Modeled after the primary governance structure described earlier, we created a structured process of virtual team connections with open forums, threaded topics, private teams, and direct messages. We then added file sharing and mobility, which included having access to this communication tool from desktops, tablets, and easily accessible mobile applications that allowed voting options. The entire governance group (including the support team) was able to communicate and comment as they did in live meetings, with the voting physicians casting their approval or disapproval of pertinent change requests, updates, and enhancements at their convenience.

Taking a governance group meeting virtual is not magic, but there is a formula for making it easy for busy physicians to participate in this approach to EHR governance. It combines a deep understanding of how different types of providers are likely to engage in a conversation and making sure the subject matter is relevant to them, in the patient's best interest and benefits the organization.

This virtual governance process was piloted with a Nephrology group (Figure 10.7). They were an ideal use case because they had expressed consistent interest in participating in their EHR governance yet failed to meet quorum in their meetings month-over-month. Their chair, while not a technophile, was committed to finding a solution. This worked to the advantage of the pilot since his feedback regarding the virtual governance process was specific and targeted issues that may have been overlooked by others more technologically inclined. His group's success on the platform was the impetus other groups needed to give it a try.

Welcome to the private team **CCG - Nephrology**! *Online forum for Change Request discussion and voting*

Figure 10.7 One nephrology governance group transitions its EHR governance meetings onto a virtual platform.

All members of the Nephrology decision-body group – physician, nursing, support informatics, etc. – were invited into the virtual governance group platform. Since this was fundamentally a communication platform, this allowed everyone to see and share comments. However, only the voting members were allowed to record approval or disapproval using the thumbs up or thumbs down emoticon. Each change request under discussion was posted as its own topic preventing overlapping conversations on different change request tickets. The title of the topic was the change request ticket number from our defect management system and the name of the request. The group's facilitator posted the change request under consideration into the platform, spelling out the business case and sharing pertinent supporting documentation (similar to what was done in agendas for our regular meetings). At the bottom of the post was a requested *vote by* date, usually five to seven business days later unless there was a pressing need to expedite the process (Figure 10.8). Posting a topic automatically notified all members of the virtual governance group of a new request. Any member of the group could then comment (or vote, for the voting members) at their convenience.

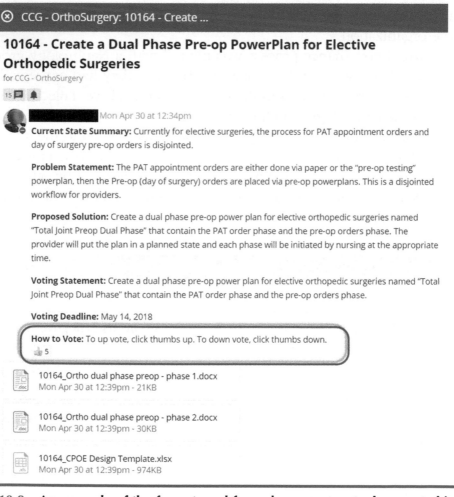

Figure 10.8   An example of the format used for a change request when posted into a virtual platform.

If a request was modified or approved, the title was updated to reflect this.

Within a year of initiating this pilot, two of our specialty-specific groups (nephrology and orthopedics) were using a virtual platform exclusively for their EHR governance needs. No more canceled meetings month-over-month due to a lack of quorum. And five more groups used a virtual platform to occasionally replace or supplement their live meetings. This included our two largest physician decision body governance groups, each with well over 150 members. Their normal two-week cadence between meetings was cut by more than 50% with most expedited change requests posted in the virtual platform being voted upon within 72 hours. This platform was also adopted by an Oncology *best practice* group to provide rapid approval for their expedited oncology regimen governance (Figure 10.9).

Figure 10.9   The oncology best practice group adopts a virtual platform to supplement their in-person meetings and partner with EHR governance.

The greatest challenge to taking governance virtual is buy-in and adoption across the full spectrum of providers. Shifting large groups of people into a virtual communication platform requires patience and persistence. Creating a structured process that is intuitive makes it easier to champion and socialize this approach. And, as with most new technology processes, once a critical core of (early) adopters are on board, others follow either out of a new level of comfort or peer pressure.

Another challenge encountered was managing complex change requests on a virtual platform. The goal was to have the change request be self-evident and to the extent possible, anticipate any questions a provider may have. To do this, we started requesting a short video (that we posted as part of the business case) in support of change requests with multiple parts or a certain level of complexity. Of course, all groups using a virtual platform for governance were monitored regularly for questions, concerns, and feedback. Responses, where appropriate, were provided within one business day.

Taking an EHR governance process virtual is a big deal that, when done correctly, offers many benefits and rewards. Prior to selecting a platform, you first need to have a clear idea of where you're going, why you're doing it, and how this is going to benefit the organization. Start with one clinical group that has a problem that a virtual governance methodology can solve. Work with them for four to six months in a rapid iterative style to instantiate a process that can be scaled to others. Once you have a solid 1.0 version process, expand and embrace continual refinement based on input and feedback from your expanding group of key stakeholders. As is often the case, the devil is in the details. There must be continual monitoring of the platform and timely responses to inquiries and postings. The look and feel of the platform needs to be consistent and standardized.

Chapter Summary

- Once you've successfully optimized one or several parts of your EHR governance processes, automate by finding opportunities to perform structured, repetitive processes with minimal human assistance.
- Scaling EHR processes to other groups in your organization (e.g., pharmacy, quality, CDI) is another way to consolidate gains and produce more wins.
- Consider a virtual asynchronous communication platform for EHR governance groups that have difficulty meeting and achieving a quorum.

Chapter Exercises

If you are developing a new EHR governance strategy for your organization, it will be a year or two until you've had a few wins and matured enough to start thinking about how to consolidate your gains. If you are refining an existing EHR governance structure and feel ready for this step, focus on the tasks that you've optimized that are highly standardized and repetitive. While several examples were provided in this chapter, you and your team will likely have a short list of possible projects to tackle. Write them down. Discuss which one (or two) you would prioritize and when you might be ready to take it on.

Chapter 11

Anchor New Approaches in the Culture

We are what we repeatedly do. Excellence then, is not an act, but a habit.

– Aristotle

After a few years of challenging work and several successfully executed projects, it is tempting to declare victory and rest on your laurels. While we're all for celebrating wins, declaring the war won may be catastrophic. Until your EHR governance processes become part of the organizational culture, they are fragile and subject to regression. Expect this to take between five and ten years – maybe longer.

Culture Eats Strategy for Breakfast

I must admit, I never used to pay much attention to culture. I knew it was there and I had read enough to know of its profound impact on the ability of change to stick. Honestly, I thought of it much like gravity. The effects of it were plain to see yet it was hard to quantify – elusive, stable background noise. That may seem naive since the teams I've worked with over the years were strong, passionate souls driven by a mission to transform the user experience. Culturally we tended to be straight talking, hardworking evangelists who were uncomfortable with too much adulation or deference,

DOI: 10.4324/9781003008408-13

refrained from engaging in too much bureaucracy and were always on the hunt for creative, out-of-the-box solutions. Often showered with praise, we seemed untouchable. Then, one day, in one of the larger organizations I worked with, it all went sideways.

On the cusp of a merger with a much larger organization, a senior team leader announced that he would be leaving a few weeks later to take a dream job. When I heard this news, the ground shifted beneath me. Much of the team's identity was tied to this single, well-positioned, charismatic leader and for the first time the team's continued support and success concerned me. Management of the team was transitioned to my bosses' boss, who also left one month later. After losing two leaders within as many months, without a clear plan of succession or transition, the team rallied internally, working diligently to maintain a tightly aligned strategy that demonstrated value, while the world around us merged and reorganized. As a team nourished by a diet of high transparency and communication, the lack of information from our leadership on what our future looked like was devastating. Over the next few months, a key anchor for the team was part of a reduction in force; several other team members, seeing the writing on the wall, left to join new organizations; and the remaining team members were transitioned internally. In less than a year, a highly functioning governance team had been dissolved and many of the organization's governance processes were frozen for reevaluation or transition. Culture had eaten strategy for breakfast.

Culture is the intersection between how people interact with one another and how they respond to change, which results in a set of behavioral norms and shared values. It's easy to be unaware of culture because it's everywhere, making it invisible, hard to address, and challenging to change. Although rarely stated or documented, culture has a powerful influence on human behavior. Culture is tacit and feels squishy, but as former General Electric CEO Jack Welch once famously said, *the soft stuff is the hard stuff.*

Strategy, on the other hand, is a high-level plan to achieve one or more goals. It involves determining actions to achieve those goals and mobilizing resources to execute the actions. Most organizations have a clearly defined strategy that can span multiple years. Strategy is often captured in a document; definable and knowable. The solid nature of strategy makes it feel reliable and dependable. However, the ubiquitous nature of culture is a double-edged sword that can either enhance strategy or destroy it. Let's see why.

Whether overtly stated or not, cultural norms are deeply woven into the fabric of every organization. They play a huge role in the hiring and retention process. Many job descriptions give a brief description of company culture as a way of attracting people of like mind. This is especially true in organizations where the culture is a major part of the brand. For example, the culture at Amazon is conveyed as being intense and innovative whereas Zappos is known for being the customer-focused kingdom of happiness. In both cases, culture is a key part of the brand which will ultimately attract a certain type of person seeking a job. In this way, culture is self-preserving and self-perpetuating. Hires that challenge cultural norms can introduce a fresh perspective and innovation when empowered to do so. However, if a disrupter makes it through the hiring process and is not converted to the culture they find themselves in, they may not last long.

Culture also plays a more subliminal role in onboarding and indoctrinating people into an organization or team. This power is exerted through the joint consciousness and consensus of large numbers of people. These are the unspoken values and expectations of the organization which ideally are aligned to the spoken value. One example, close to home, was my onboarding experience when I accepted a position as the Medical Director for Health Informatics in a large healthcare organization. My boss spent approximately 20 hours in the first few weeks of my employment carefully walking me through team strategy and dynamics, anticipating and answering any questions that I had. Engagement with the larger team reinforced these social norms again and again. In my entire medical career, I've never had this detailed level of onboarding by an executive, which impressed upon me the gravity and expectations of the work. I didn't realize it at the time, but cultural expectations were being clearly set from day one.

Since culture usually develops and evolves without conscious intent, it becomes difficult to challenge, shift, or discuss. How do you anchor change in an environment that you can't easily define? The good news is that you don't need to understand all the nuances of a culture to find ways to anchor change and shift it. Here are some suggestions:

- Communicate Early and Often. Leaders need to clearly describe the values and behaviors they're seeking. Over communicating this message is not possible.
- Align Strategy and Culture. This includes core values, hiring processes, incentives, accountability, etc. Be clear about what is non-negotiable.

Over the long horizon, this also entails having a plan of succession that guarantees that hardwon change gets carried forward.

■ Leaders Need to Lead: Get buy-in from the C-suite and key influencers.
■ Align Culture and Brand. Remember, in some of the most successful organizations, the culture is the brand.
■ Measure What Matters. Tracking data metrics to inform progress is key to reinforcing organizational priorities.
■ Land and Expand. Don't sacrifice the good for the perfect; that is, don't wait until your change is fully baked before you start. Once you have a viable process, deploy (land) with the understanding that you will continue to expand and refine.
■ Buckle Up. Cultural change takes time because you must influence people's actions and incentivize new behaviors to enhance performance. Be patient. Be persistent. Be vigilant.

Nurture your EHR governance process early on when it is fragile and vulnerable. This means watching for signs that the underlying culture is reasserting itself and addressing incompatibilities as they arise. Culture evolves over time and is created by the behavior you tolerate.

Culture Styles

While we've just described culture as a confounding, hard-to-define, yet powerful force that can either synergize or destroy your EHR governance change efforts, this does an injustice to a large body of social science literature that suggests that culture can not only be understood, it can also be managed. Well-respected voices in this space include seminal work by Edgar Schein, Shalom Schwartz, and Geert Hofstede as well as more contemporary perspectives by researchers such as Robert Quinn and Kim Cameron. In 2018, Harvard Business School Professor Boris Groysberg and his colleagues, Jeremiah Lee, Jesse Price and J, Yo-Jud Cheng, built upon this work by introducing a framework based upon their analysis of data on culture from over 230 companies along with the leadership styles and values of more than 1,300 executives across a range of industries, regions, and organizational types.[1] This framework was organized around variation across the spectrum of how people interact and how they respond to change. Eight distinct cultural styles emerged: caring, purpose, learning, enjoyment, results, authority, safety, and order (Figure 11.1).

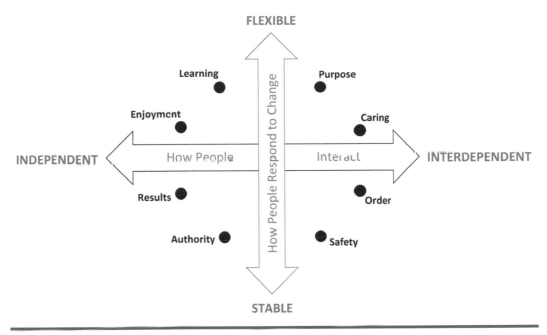

Figure 11.1 **A depiction of the eight culture styles that emerge based on how people interact and how people respond to change: purpose, caring, order, safety, authority, results, enjoyment, and learning.** Source: Adapted from the work of *https://hbr.org/2018 /01/the-leaders-guide-to-corporate-culture.*

A caring culture values relationships and mutual trust. These are the companies where employees are united by feelings of collaboration and loyalty. The atmosphere is warm and welcoming. People have a sense of belonging. The potential downside to a caring culture is that it can dampen innovation and the desire for consensus may slow decision making. Disney is an example of a caring culture.

A culture driven by purpose values idealism and altruism. These are companies where employees are passionate about making a difference in the world, contributing to the greater good. The atmosphere is tolerant and compassionate. The potential downside to a purpose-driven culture is that long-term impact may get in the way of immediate concerns. Whole Foods is an example of an organization driven by purpose.

A learning culture values being open, inventive, and creative. These are companies where employees are united by curiosity and adventure. The atmosphere is innovative and open-minded. The potential downside to a learning culture is a lack of focus and the inability to exploit current opportunities. Tesla is an example of a learning culture.

A culture of enjoyment values light-heartedness and doing what makes them happy. These are companies where employees are united by spontaneity and a sense of humor. The atmosphere is playful and fun. The potential downside to a culture of enjoyment is a lack of discipline leading to compliance and governance issues. Zappos is an example of an organization driven by a culture of enjoyment.

A results culture values achievement and winning. These are companies where employees are incentivized and results driven. The atmosphere is competitive and goal oriented. The potential downside to a results culture is poor collaboration and increased stress or anxiety. GlaxoSmithKline is an example of a results culture.

A culture of authority values bold decision and strong authority. These are companies where employees compete and work to gain personal advantage. The atmosphere is decisive and confident. The potential downside to a culture of authority is politics, conflict, and a psychologically unsafe work environment. Chinese tech company Huawei is an example of a culture of authority.

A safety culture values being realistic, careful, and prepared. These are companies where employees think things through carefully and strive to reduce risk. The atmosphere is cautious and predictable. The potential downside to a safety culture is bureaucracy, inflexibility, and dehumanization of the work environment. Lloyds of London is an example of a safety culture.

And finally, an order culture values abiding by the rules, structure and tradition. These are companies where employees are methodical and want to fit in. The atmosphere is respectful and efficient. The potential downside to an order culture is that it may dampen creativity, reduce individualism, or limit organizational agility. The US Securities and Exchange Commission (SEC) is an example of an order culture.

Healthcare organizations usually have a mixture of cultural styles, with some being more dominant than others. The care delivery part of your organization probably has a predominant culture of safety, caring, or purpose (Figure 11.2). The research arm of your organization may have a culture focused on results, while the digital and innovation team probably values a culture of learning. Boris Groysberg and his colleagues offer a worksheet *https://hbr.org/2018/01/whats-your-organizations-cultural-profile?ab =seriesnav-spotlight* that allows you to generate a complete cultural profile of your organization. It's a good idea to have a few different people in your organization complete the profile to see if the perceived culture style is

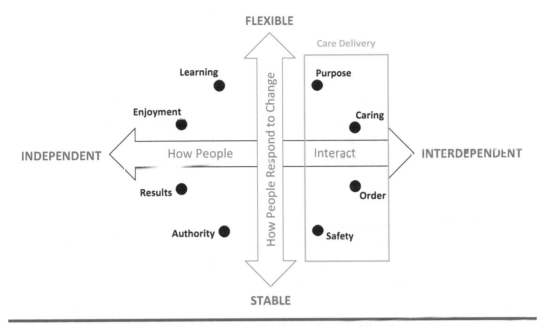

Figure 11.2 The culture style of healthcare delivery organizations tends to be more purpose, caring, order, and safety focused. Biomedical researchers are often results focused. Source: Adapted from the work of *https://hbr.org/2018/01/the-leaders-guide-to -corporate-culture.*

the same or similar across the organization. When there is concordance of culture style across an organization, that culture is quite strong and likely a strong influencer of your brand. The downside to this strong alignment is that introducing any change that shifts the culture may be met with more resistance. On the flip side, an organization that is perceived by its employees as having several different culture styles may be more amenable to change, especially when it provides a unifying vision.

Once you understand your current state culture style profile, the conversation can begin. What are your strengths? Is your culture aligned to your EHR governance strategy? If not, how will you pivot to have them align with or complement one another? We will explore this further in an exercise at the end of the chapter.

The Way We Do Things around Here

How do you know when your EHR governance processes have become woven into the DNA of your organization? When have hearts and minds been won over? When can you declare that *we're done* and it's safe to say *this is the way we do things around here*? It's common to want answers to these questions because our linear brain craves change models that are modular and measurable. First we do *A*, then we do *B*, and success is when we reach *C*. We feel a certain sense of accomplishment when we can put a check in the EHR governance check box. We've finally crossed the finish line. The problem is this isn't how it really works. Change isn't linear and doesn't occur in a vacuum. Within a single organization, multiple change initiatives are unfolding concurrently competing for time, acceptance, and resources. Success comes from building something new that makes the existing model obsolete; build the better mouse trap; innovate, innovate, and innovate – but never think in terms of being done.

There are two aspects to anchoring change in a culture, the thinking piece and the emotional piece. We've discussed many aspects of the thinking piece throughout the book but let's recap some of the highlights that are so appealing to our logical brains. Showcase the data demonstrating the superiority of your new governance change processes and clearly explain the benefits they bring; keep it simple and easy to understand. Identify the norms and values that support the new change and make sure they are a good fit with the culture. Ensure selection, promotion, and succession processes that identify talent who align with the new way of doing things. Make sure rewards and incentives reinforce the new culture. Adjust training and development activities to develop the skills and competencies associated with supporting and growing your new governance processes. Reassign or remove employees and managers who are attached to the old way of doing things and barriers to the progress the organization has made. Remember, culture and leadership are inextricably linked. Founders and influential leaders have the power to establish new cultural norms and imprint values that can persist for decades. The best leaders are cognizant of their ability to do this and can skillfully influence the process.

The second aspect, the emotional piece, is a different story. This is the piece that is often deeply ingrained in stories and experiences making it harder to shift but a more powerful lever for anchoring lasting change. Remember, every change costs someone something so it pays to be sensitive to the common emotions experienced with any new change. Some people experience fear because change takes you into something unknown, and the unknown is scary for almost everyone. Retraining may be required which can push people out of their comfort zone and make them feel insecure about the future. Others may grieve the loss of a routine or habit that they've grown accustomed to. The enthusiastic group who embraces change may frustrate and antagonize those experiencing pain or loss. Anger is not uncommon among those who had ownership in the old way of doing things. Confusion often affects those who strive to learn a new way of doing things, while others react to a learning curve with loneliness or sadness. And when change is rapid, some people just withdraw and become unresponsive, not knowing exactly what to feel.

This emotional part of your brain is more primitive and powerful; it is imprinted by things that evoke emotion such as role modeling, storytelling, and experiences; things that leave an impression upon your heart. Maya Angelou expressed this phenomenon succinctly in her famous quote: *At the end of the day people won't remember what you said or did, they will remember how you made them feel.*

Emotional intelligence is the bridge that connects your thinking brain and your emotional brain. People with high emotional intelligence are more adaptable, inquisitive, and see great value in learning from both their successes and failures. Emotional intelligence makes us less rigid and resistant, helping us to learn, adapt, and innovate. If this isn't the way you are wired, don't worry, emotional intelligence is a skill that can be learned. *Harvard Business Review* authors Kandi Wiens and Darin Rowell offer four strategies for developing emotional intelligence:[2]

First, identify the source of your discomfort. This requires a modicum of self-awareness; you must be able to look at yourself and assess the underlying cause of your feelings with some level of objectivity. Perhaps you see the change being adopted requires skills that you don't currently have. You worry about your viability and fear for your job. However, recognition is dissolution, meaning that once you identify the problem, remediating it becomes much easier. In this case you might seek direction on what skills to develop and apply yourself accordingly. Or maybe you're concerned about your autonomy. In that case, see about becoming more involved. Identify yourself as a team player and give the new process the benefit of the doubt.

The second strategy entails questioning the basis of your emotional response. Perhaps you have an old story or a series of old stories playing on a loop in your head that you are convinced are true. These stories are usually colored by personal biases and perspectives. This is usually easy enough to discern if you investigate further. First, identify the primary emotion you are dealing with. Is it fear, anger, grief, or something else? It may be tempting to say *all of the above*, but the more specific you can be, the easier it will be to identify the *why* behind your beliefs and the emotion you are experiencing.

For example, when my boss announced that he was leaving to take a new position, I was scared. I was afraid of the lack of a succession plan; I was afraid the team would be set adrift; I was afraid of who might step in to fill his shoes. I went home and sat with my fear and discovered that I felt powerless; a victim to the impending change. I wasn't the only one feeling this way. My boss, sensing this, gathered the team together a day or two later and read us this quote from Buddhist nun and author Pema Chodron:

> In life we think that the point is to pass the test or overcome the problem. The real truth is that things don't really get solved. They come together for a time, then they fall back apart. Then they come together and fall apart again. It's just like that.
>
> Personal discovery and growth come from letting there be room for all this to happen: room for grief, for relief, for misery, for joy.
>
> Suffering comes from wishing things were different. Misery is self-inflicted, when we are expecting the "idea" to overcome the "actual," or needing things (or people, or places) to be different for us so we can then be happy.
>
> Let the hard things in life break you. Let them affect you. Let them change you. Let those hard moments inform you. Let this pain be your teacher. The experiences of your life are trying to tell you something about yourself. Don't cop out on that. Don't run away and hide under your covers. Lean into it.
> What is the lesson in the wind? What is the storm trying to tell you? What will you learn if you face it with courage? With full honesty and – lean into it.

Truth is, while that quote had an immediately soothing effect upon me, it challenged me to be flexible; to change; to see a bigger picture. In that moment, everything was going to be okay.

The third strategy is to own your part in the situation. Stated another way, when you identify a problem, a key place to look for the cause is in the mirror. This is counterintuitive for most of us having been born and raised in a culture that typically identifies external factors as causative agents. However, almost every response you make in a situation has a personal payoff. This may include being identified as the poor victim who was wronged; or the savvy negotiator who got the better end of the deal; or the resilient leader who stood strong through the turmoil. It's not always easy to fess up to the part we play, even if it is subtle, in creating a negative situation. However, your muscles of emotional intelligence get flexed when you take the time to reflect on how your attitudes and behaviors contribute to the experience of change. The emotionally intelligent recognize the power of their thoughts and actions in creating their reality and modulate them accordingly.

The final of the four strategies is to look on the bright side. This may sound disingenuous if you don't agree with the change at hand, but this is an age-old secret that opens you to new ways of thinking and makes you more receptive to change. The optimist sees the possibility in everything; she listens; she reflects; she discriminates. This is not to be confused with having a Pollyanna mind set where everything is rose-colored and perfect. Finding ways to think optimistically when it comes to EHR governance change isn't hard. Your guiding coalition and other change agents are already broadcasting all the positive things that the new EHR governance processes have done or will do. Choose those things that resonate with you and become a champion of them. In this way you will build your flexibility and reputation as an agent of change. This provides a competitive advantage for all, but especially for leaders.

All changes weave their way through varying stages of chaos and homeostasis. High chaos means change is happening. Sometimes that simply means learning. If change doesn't work, homeostasis sets in as we metaphorically catch our breath and then we start the cycle all over again. Remember, it's not linear. Communicate often, clearly, and consistently; this is not a project; this is not a program; this is the new way of doing things. It has stuck when the old way of doing things is largely forgotten.

Chapter Summary

- Culture is the intersection between how people interact with one another and how they respond to change, which results in a set of behavioral norms and shared values.
- If not aligned, culture has the power to undermine your EHR governance processes.
- Changing cultural norms and expectations takes time so prepare to be patient, persistent, and vigilant.
- The social science literature suggests that culture can be measured and managed. Eight distinct cultural styles discussed include: caring, purpose, learning, enjoyment, results, authority, safety, and order.
- When it comes to EHR governance processes, there is no finish line.
- Logic and emotion anchor change. Emotional intelligence is the bridge between the two:
    - When you are uncomfortable, find the source of your discomfort.
    - Question the basis of your emotional response.
    - Own your part in the situation.
    - Look on the bright side.

Chapter Exercises

The goal of this exercise is to discover if the existing culture in your health-care system is going to readily enable your EHR governance strategy or not. What culture do you really have – remembering that who people are and what they truly believe are most revealed when uncomfortable or under pressure? Culture is key because it can nullify or destroy the best EHR governance strategy.

1. What's your organization's cultural style profile? Harvard Business Professor Boris Groysberg and his colleagues offer a worksheet *https://hbr.org/2018/01/whats-your-organizations-cultural-profile?ab=seriesnav-spotlight* that will allow you to generate a complete cultural profile of your organization. It's a good idea to have a few different people in your organization complete the profile to see if the perceived culture style is the same or similar across the organization.
2. Once you understand your current state culture style profile, assess your strengths. Is your culture aligned to your EHR governance strategy? If not, how will you pivot to have them align with or complement one another? Frame your answers to this question as an organizational change priority that you can act upon.

COMMITMENT

3

You're not obligated to win. You're obligated to keep trying to do the best you can every day.

– Marian Wright Edelman

DOI: 10.4324/9781003008408-14

Chapter 12

User Experience

The real problem is not whether machines think but whether men do.

– B.F. Skinner

People, Process, and Technology

This book is squarely focused on an EHR governance model driven by user experience – that is, as a robust provider documentation tool and a vehicle for collaborative patient engagement. However, the voice of the end user has been lost in a sea of other emboldened stakeholders who expect the EHR to be and do more. Insurance companies want accurate, efficient authorization processes; pharmacies seek seamless, real-time eprescribing; legislative and regulatory mandates require a growing number of metrics be collected and reported; public health officials want surveillance capabilities; researchers expect a clinical trials interface; innovators see a vehicle for saving the world; lawyers mine a treasure trove of discoverable data; and so on. The EHR has evolved into a servant of many masters with the unintended consequence of burdening the very physicians and patients it should be focused upon serving. While a foreign concept within the healthcare industry, the idea of the end user(s) driving the development and optimization of a software tool has a long and well-respected history.

In 1964, the Information Technology Infrastructure Library (ITIL)[1] introduced the people, process, and technology framework as a model for organizational transformation. Adopted from Harold Leavitt's 1964 paper *Applied*

DOI: 10.4324/9781003008408-15

Organizational Change in Industry and later referred to simply as the three-legged stool or the golden triangle, the theory stressed a proper balance between people, process, and technology to ensure successful change. That balance included a particular emphasis on the people part of the model, noting that the absence of the right people with the right attitude, practical experience, and qualifications would ensure failure.[2] It warned that concentrating only on the technology would result in a wobbly stool.

In 2018, Christopher Penn modernized this model to better reflect an era of rapid technological growth.[3] Instead of a stool or a triangle, Mr. Penn reimagined people, process, and technology as equal and interdependent parts of a dynamic relationship, whose intersections form the momentum for innovation, automation, and scalability (Figure 12.1).

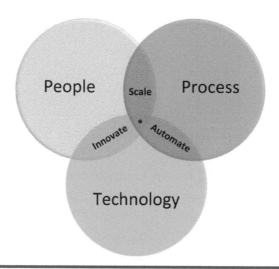

Figure 12.1 **People, process, and technology as equal and interdependent parts of a dynamic relationship whose intersections form the momentum for innovation, automation, and scalability.** Source: Adapted from Christopher Penn, Transforming People, Process, and Technology – Christopher S. Penn – Marketing Data Science Keynote Speaker (*christopherspenn.com*).

People and technology intersect to drive innovation; technology and process intersect to drive automation; people and process intersect to drive scalability. The alignment of all three, people, process, and technology, is a guaranteed win. This way of thinking about the golden triangle framework quickly expands how we define and apply EHR governance processes. While design work remains the heart of what we do, we know that work cannot be done in a silo. We marry the platform enhancement to the correct workflow for the right people. We innovate, automate, and scale. We partner in comprehensive scenario-based and regression testing. We engage in crisp communication, providing enough lead time to socialize changes and offer support. In short, we look at the process end-to-end with the understanding that even the best design deployed without these other considerations will fail. In fact, evidence suggests that the technology may be the least impactful component of the model in determining EHR success and satisfaction. The most important factor, as emphasized by the developers of the original framework 55 years ago, continues to be people. The successful adoption of the EHR begins and ends with the people using it.

This expanded way of thinking dovetails perfectly with the interdependent three Ds model (define, design, discover) presented in Chapter 3. EHR changes are designed in response to the work done by groups who establish best practice standards. Instead of documenting to fill in all the boxes or to meet coding-level requirements, you capture critical, meaningful information that tells the patient's story, key clinical findings, an assessment, and a plan of care. You transition from the *if it wasn't documented, it wasn't done* mindset to focusing on the meaningful transfer of knowledge. This becomes the expectation when EHR governance design work is driven by and optimized to user experience. You leverage technology tools such as health information exchange, telehealth, and patient portals; technology doesn't leverage you.

Now, instead of seeing the IT team as a group of non-clinicians finessing the nuts and bolts of a software platform, you see their attention to how flagging an abnormal test result in a red font was designed purposefully to improve the physician's ability to recognize abnormal test results quickly and deliver better patient care. You see how the elegant design of placing CDS alerts into a passive sidebar was intended to reduce physician disruption while keeping key data available to inform decisions. The design and development of multi-contributory documentation purposefully allows all members of the healthcare team to participate in developing a comprehensive set of instructions to accompany the patient at discharge. Ambient voice technology captures the physician–patient conversation at a high level of fidelity and seamlessly generates a succinct note to free the physician to engage more fully with the patient. It is challenging, in fact, to come up with an example where a technology platform change isn't driven by or impactful to some underlying group of people or processes.

HIT priorities are developed in response to organizational goals, end user input, and strategic alignments. Software owners determine product roadmaps in a similar fashion, responding to regulations and user feedback while innovating to maintain market share in a competitive landscape. To be successful, EHR governance processes must be agile, aligned, and attentive to the interdependencies between the people, the processes, and the technology.

The KLAS Arch Collaborative

KLAS Research[4] conducted its first studies of EHR usability in 2012 and published its first EHR usability report in 2013. Although EHRs had been around for many years prior, the infusion of $30 billion into the healthcare system from the 2009 Health Information Technology for Economic and Clinical Health (HITECH) Act accelerated EHR adoption by many organizations. KLAS wanted to understand how EHR usability varied between and within healthcare organizations and if there were differences from vendor to vendor. To collect this data, KLAS interviewed approximately 150 healthcare professionals, including Chief Information Officers (CIOs) and Chief Medical Information Officers (CMIOs), to capture their experience and perception of how their EHR was functioning, with a specific emphasis on system onboarding, usability, and efficiency. This provided baseline information on system maturation and optimization.

KLAS expected to find similar practices employed by organizations who had successfully deployed an EHR. But responses from organizational leaders were variable, and many were non-specific about the perceived experience of the provider (e.g., *I think the usability was satisfactory*). In response, KLAS repeated the initial 2013 usability study every two years to track improvement. Progress in fixing a lot of the issues identified was anticipated but wasn't found. Just the opposite, EHR challenges seemed to intensify, despite significant technology development work from both vendors and provider organizations.

Additional data analyses identified a gap where organizations were not getting feedback from one key EHR stakeholder – the provider. In fact, less than 7% of organizations interviewed by KLAS had formally surveyed their providers regarding their EHR experience. KLAS recognized the need and opportunity to step in to provide a standardized survey that would benchmark provider responses across organizations and identify areas of strengths and weaknesses. This was the origin of the KLAS Arch Collaborative.[5]

The Arch Collaborative methodology was designed to establish a measure of EHR user experience that could be benchmarked within and between organizations. The core survey was comprised of 35 questions with multiple components and conditional logic. Survey questions ascertained user demographics (e.g., specialty, experience, location), experience with initial and ongoing training, EHR personalization tools used, documentation practices and perceptions about how well the vendor, the organization, and the users themselves supported the EHR. Questions were piloted with early participants in the Collaborative and validated by focus groups conducted by KLAS.

The main metric used to measure user experience was a composite score called the Net EHR Experience Score (NEES), which was likened to a net promoter score. The NEES was calculated from responses to 11 questions with 5 Likert-scale choices ranging from Strongly Agree to Strongly Disagree.

Do you agree with the following statements? This EHR ...

- enables me to deliver high-quality care
- makes me as efficient as possible
- is available when I need it (has almost no downtime)
- has the functionality I expect
- provides the integration within our organization I expect
- provides the integration with outside organizations I expect
- has the fast system response time I expect
- is easy to learn
- provides the analytics and reporting I need
- keeps my patients safe
- allows me to deliver patient-centered care

The NEES represented the percentage of negative user feedback subtracted from the percentage of positive user feedback, ranging from −100% (all negative feedback) to +100% (all positive feedback).

KLAS used correlation tables and multiple linear regression to identify which factors had the largest effect on the NEES. They also analyzed the decomposition of the variation of the NEES across the Collaborative. To do this, the average absolute difference of the NEES was calculated sequentially across the different EHR vendors, organizations, and specialties and among the individuals. Percent of variation at each level was calculated using the average absolute difference of each level divided by the sum of differences. Similar methods have been used to decompose variation using a variety of statistical parameters. Their findings surprised many: 60% of the variation in EHR satisfaction was attributable to the clinician end user (people), 18% from the organization (process) and 22% from the EHR vendor (technology) (Figures 12.2 and 12.3).

Where Does the Variation Come From?

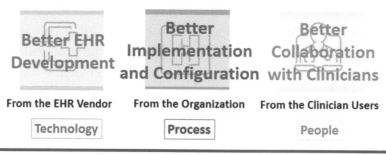

Figure 12.2   **The major sources of variation in EHR satisfaction come from the clinician end user (people), the organization (process), and the EHR vendor (technology).** Source: Data from the KLAS Arch Collaborative.

Where Does the Variation Come From?

Figure 12.3   **Sixty percent of the variation in EHR satisfaction is attributed to the clinician end user, 18% to the organization, and 22% from the EHR vendor.** Source: Data from the KLAS Arch Collaborative.

Additional analyses and several follow-back studies have allowed the Arch Collaborative to verify several best practices in support of an improved EHR user experience. They include service-oriented support, engaging training, proactive interoperability, personalization of user settings and interface, and an efficient EHR governance structure with a mechanism for making rapid changes when required.

Service-Oriented Support: Any successful service model must recognize that EHR end users are highly-skilled, highly-trained, well-paid professionals. Engaging them in drawn-out, time-consuming processes when something requires fixing or optimization within the EHR is a sure-fire way to frustrate and alienate. Take, for example, the typical process required to call in a help desk ticket. The first minute or two is typically spent painstakingly confirming your identity, location, and specialty. Then it's on to describing your problem. Many help desk services are outsourced so sometimes you are speaking to someone in China, India, or the Philippines with an accent that is challenging to understand. *Do you have a screenshot or a record identifier that you can share to help reproduce and troubleshoot the problem?* Then comes the follow-up email or emails with your ticket number and further information, as appropriate. And, finally, the email request comes asking you to rate your customer experience with the help desk interaction. Many physicians, after going through a process like this once or twice, vow to never call the help desk again – ever. There are organizations, however, appreciating the cost both monetarily and mentally of such a process on their physicians, that have adopted different models. Some have a dedicated support service number for physician use. Some have insourced to vendor-supported services. Others have relayed these requests directly to their internal informatics team or developed apps to streamline the experience. Regardless of what was done, the goal was always to remove the friction that the end user experiences when requesting help to fix something.

Engaging Training: You get one opportunity to get initial provider EHR training right. This is a top priority if you have a go live on the horizon. Training is most effective when it is targeted, timely, workflow driven, personalized, and offers CME/CEU. This should be reinforced with at-the-elbow support during go live to establish the best practices and workflows possible. However, once the go live is over and the command center closes, the need for training doesn't disappear; that is, EHR training is not a one-and-done deal. As we'll discuss in the next section, the opportunities to update and optimize your EHR will continue as will the need to keep providers up-to-date. This need for ongoing training has been approached by healthcare organizations in different ways. Kaiser Permanente Northwest, for example, created the *Pathways to Proficiency* program. Three times a year, 195 physicians are relieved from their normal day-to-day clinical work for a three-day immersion; they attend an off-site meeting where they spend uninterrupted time improving their EHR efficiency. This training also qualifies for Category 1 CME credit.

Proactive Interoperability: Interoperability was the great promise of nationwide EHR adoption. The reality to date has fallen short of the hype but several efforts are underway to correct that. In fact, on March 9, 2020, the Department of Health & Human Services officially released the next phase of the 21st Century Cures Act, the interoperability rule, primarily focusing on interoperability and patient information blocking. The goal here was to foster interoperability through data sharing and identify activities that do not constitute information blocking. The rules also increase choices and competition while promoting innovation to expand patient access to and control over their health information.

Personalization Use: Refining the way your EHR software works to better align with the way a provider works is key to a satisfying user experience. Using personalization tools and setting filters to optimize workflow for a care team translates into more effective, efficient care delivery. One organization approached this proactively by having provider informaticists round two times a month. This process acknowledged that providers are often too busy to report problems, set filters, or at times aren't aware that there may be better ways to do something. Instead, they muddle through creating workarounds that may take more time and effort to get the job done or just suffer silently. These rounding interactions help mitigate that problem and, more importantly, build rapport and relationships by letting providers experience how the informatics team is actively working to make their job easier. In larger organizations or where there is geographic distancing between locations, this may be achieved much of the time, virtually.

Efficient Governance Structure: The data collected worldwide through the KLAS Arch Collaborative supports the provider-centric, consensus-driven model of EHR governance detailed in this book. That is, to be successful, EHR governance must embrace the voice of the end user; it must be fair, equitable, and transparent; it must be representative and responsive; and it must align well to best-practice workflows. It must also have an expedited change request process when time is of the essence. The appropriate use of this pathway must be well-defined and documented so it is not susceptible to misuse or abuse.

The Arch Collaborative data, together with their verified best practices, teaches us that variation in physician EHR user experience is due largely to a combination of people- and process-related issues, followed by technology-related issues. People-related factors include initial onboarding and ongoing training for mastery within the EHR and the physician's use of personalization tools such as templates, filters, preference lists, and order sets. Process-related factors include physician engagement in their EHR governance processes, workflow coordination, and optimization. This leaves about a third of the variation seen in the NEES attributable to the EHR platform technology itself.

While EHR vendors must continue to improve their systems with a focus on usability, organizations don't have to wait on vendors to improve their physicians' EHR experience. By having a strategy that is focused on people and process, organizations can support and assist physicians to have a better experience with their EHR now. That's exactly what OrthoVirginia did – with great success.

OrthoVirginia (OV) is an orthopedic specialty group comprised of over 1,500 employees, 121 physicians, 99 Advanced Practice Providers and 176 therapy providers delivering care in 26 locations across the state of Virginia. OV first participated in the Arch Collaborative in September of 2017 and achieved a NEES of 11%, which placed them in the 31st percentile. They remeasured in October of 2018 and earned a NEES of 55%, which placed them in the 78th percentile. They last measured in January 2020 and were surprised to again earn a NEES of 58%. When they stratified the data, they identified that therapy providers (OT/PT), as a subgroup, reported a poorer EHR experience. When they were separated out, the remainder of the provider group had achieved a NEES of 68%.

As OV's CMIO H.C. Eschenroeder recounted his organization's journey, he humbly cautioned that *OV is a minnow in a big ocean.* However, orthopedic EHR users are among the most dissatisfied of all medical specialties. Understanding how OV achieved repeated improvements in EHR user experience is a noteworthy case study.

In their first Arch Collaborative measurement, OV uncovered three problems their providers were facing:

1. Providers reported lacking knowledge of the EHR.
2. Advanced functionality and support were inconsistent.
3. Their EHR governance program was immature.

A plan was developed that focused on provider experience and provider–patient engagement with three guiding principles: (1) optimizing communication and time spent with the patient, (2) supporting providers by saying *yes* to requests for EHR improvements with proper expectations set and (3) data collection to guide and measure improvement.

The Provider Support Specialist (PSS) team was the secret sauce of our success, said Dr. Eschenroeder. This group, comprised mostly of scribes with a solid working knowledge of the EHR and the social skills required to develop solid working relationships with providers, was strategically located throughout the practice. Initially the team served as *firefighters* which helped them build credibility and strong relationships with the providers. Once the fires were out, the PSS team transitioned to helping providers improve efficiencies. They rounded with providers and observed workflows in a non-intrusive manner, offering suggestions one-on-one, at-the-elbow, to make things work more smoothly. Today providers and their staff welcome PSS team members with questions and appreciate when they visit. The PSS program helped alleviate the first two problems (EHR knowledge and inconsistent functionality and support).

When it came to EHR governance, OV wanted to engender a founder's philosophy where the providers had a say in the direction of the EHR and were invested in making it support the way they worked. To do this, OV adopted Kaiser Permanente Northwest's *Pyramid of Change* as a model (discussed in Chapter 2) for managing and setting expectations around EHR change requests.[6] OV's PSS team served as a bridge, effectively translating the provider's need into a change request the EHR analyst could understand. Next, the PSS and analyst determined the feasibility and complexity of the requested change. Simple requests like configuration changes or broken functionality fell into the higher levels of the pyramid and were made quickly. Regulatory requests, on the other hand, were often more complex and took longer to operationalize within the EHR (a lower level on the pyramid).

This process prioritized the voice of the providers in driving EHR optimization without placing an undue burden on them to drive the actual mechanics of governance. It also set gross expectations around change management. End users now had an idea of what changes to expect quickly and what changes would take weeks-to-months to operationalize. When a physician came with a large problem that required prioritization, the physician was asked to become the physician champion for the project. This sponsorship entailed providing input into the build, tracking progress of the project, and explaining the merits of the project to fellow providers.

The OV informatics team also gave presentations at monthly regional shareholder and department meetings in each of their three regions. The goal of these presentations was to educate providers and staff about EHR requests related to patient care, workflow enhancements, and build efforts.

Onboarding New Physicians

When new physicians are hired, they go through a detailed process to have their credentials verified, obtain staff privileges, and acquire the tools they need to do their job. The latter may include obtaining a laptop, tablet, or cell phone as well as access to software for dictating notes, instant messaging colleagues, and charting patient care. Getting EHR onboarding right means timely access to a system that can be readily personalized with ongoing training and clear workflows. Getting it wrong can result in access delays with poor training and the adoption of workarounds that are hard to correct. So how do we get it right? How do we make a memorable first impression and provide a good user experience?

A team and I set out to answer that question and came up with the process depicted in Figure 12.4. It takes advantage of three areas of innovation to evolve the process of EHR onboarding. The first area was a focus on asynchronous and interactive training modalities. Educational offerings are often the perfect use case for digital innovation or disruption since they are both highly standardized and highly repetitive. Do you need to sit a person down in an instructor-led meeting for four hours to teach something or can you offer self-serve modules that deliver learning opportunities in a more digestible manner with higher retention? This is well aligned with the literature that suggests delivering information in smaller pieces in a virtual fashion leads to a much better retention curve.[7]

Figure 12.4 A model for onboarding new providers into an EHR that takes advantage of three areas of innovation: (1) asynchronous and interactive training modalities, (2) pulling information instead of pushing it, and (3) gamification. Don't miss this key opportunity to make a memorable first impression and provide a good user experience.

Second was a focus on pulling information instead of pushing it. Traditionally training pushes information in large boluses regardless of the ability to absorb and apply that information. You are trying to do something *to* people, and it is exhausting for both the instructor and the student. Pulling information, on the other hand, is fundamental to how we problem-solve, and when we seek out answers, we are more likely to remember the information.

The third and final area that we focused on was gamification. Gamification is the application of typical elements of game playing (e.g., point scoring, competition with others, rules of play) to other areas of activity, typically as an online marketing technique to encourage engagement with a product or service. It focuses on cognitive learning techniques that keep students engaged. Awards, digital badges, competitions, and in-app quests keep user interest alive and promote regular app usage without requiring a huge budget. Gamification ranges from the simple to the complex. Everyone has engaged in some form of gamification including things like your Starbucks reward app, your LinkedIn strength of profile tool, and your Apple Watch *close the rings* feature that promotes good nutrition and exercise.

With these three foundational concepts in mind, let's unpack the process depicted in Figure 12.4 step-by-step. We begin with a welcome email to our new physician explaining the EHR onboarding process. A hyperlink connects the physician to the pre-training questionnaire which confirms their role (position) within the organization and target training needs. If they already have a high level of experience with the current EHR they may choose to complete a pre-test at this point that – with a passing score – will allow them to opt out of further training. Otherwise, they are required to complete the assigned training modules at their convenience in a remote, interactive manner. Once done, they are partnered with both a colleague preceptor and a clinical informaticist and given EHR system access. Ideally the preceptor is a physician in the same specialty who can assist with personalizing the EHR interface and provide information on best practice workflows. This is important because things not optimized when a physician first starts using a new EHR rarely change without substantial effort. One organization expedited this personalization process by creating specialty-specific user interfaces (positions) that were vetted and refined by a small group of providers within that service line. This was done for all major specialties so that, for example, the hospitalist position was uniquely different from the intensivist or cardiologist positions. Another organization tackled this personalization issue by scripting a program that allowed an onboarding physician to select a seasoned EHR provider that looked like them and adopt those person's settings.

The clinical informaticist is the onboarding physician's resource for IT-related questions and is responsible for monitoring EHR metrics over the next 90 days. Establishing this CI–physician relationship from the start creates a bond of trust and shifts the role of the CI in training from task-oriented to evaluating system use with a focus on user experience. As the physician progresses, she can be acknowledged by peers or given small rewards such as a Starbucks gift card to celebrate her success.

While a process like this can offer a strong value proposition, it has several potential failure points that should be considered. First, too few resources or the wrong resources. For example, can you commit to developing online educational modules and delivering them asynchronously? Are you able to make a long-term commitment? Many organizations grow impatient quickly and scale prematurely. New ventures commandeer key skills (e.g., agile product development). Will a process like this be competing with resources from the core business? Do you have the resources to allocate for the future while also managing for today? Will this process align with the vision of other operational leaders and other initiatives? Answering these questions candidly will allow you to refine this process in a way that leverages your organization's unique capabilities and resources.

Chapter Summary

- The scope of EHR governance must extend beyond the technological aspects of the platform to be successful.
- Technology is informed by the people and processes consuming it.
- People, process, and technology are interdependent parts of a transformation model that gives rise to innovation, automation, and scalability.
- The KLAS Arch Collaborative offers tools for benchmarking user experience within and between organizations.
- Arch Collaborative data shows that the majority of variation in user experience comes from the end user (versus the processes or the platform).
- Provider-centric, consensus-driven governance is aligned with Arch Collaborative-verified best practice.
- Onboarding providers into the EHR is an opportunity to make a memorable first impression and provide a good user experience.
- Take advantage of three areas of innovation to evolve the process of EHR onboarding:
  - Asynchronous and interactive training modalities,
  - Pulling information instead of pushing it, and
  - Gamification.

Chapter Exercises

1. If you aren't familiar with the KLAS Arch Collaborative cohort, now's the time to learn more (*https://klasresearch.com/arch-collaborative*) and consider joining. Participation in the Collaborative will allow you to benchmark a series of EHR experience metrics both internally (over time) and against over 250 participating organizations worldwide.

2. Provider onboarding into the EHR is the first chance to make a memorable impression and provide a good user experience. Armed with your answers to the questions below, work with your medical staff office to develop a process that delivers high value in a friendly and engaging manner.
   - Do you have or are you able to create virtual, asynchronous EHR training modules?
   - Are there members of your staff willing to partner with new providers for one to three months to answer questions about the EHR and workflows?
   - Do you want your informatics team to track data and provide feedback to newly onboarded providers? What metrics, specifically, would be useful?
   - What incentive(s) will support and reward the newly onboarded provider in achieving a high level of proficiency within the EHR? Peer recognition? Something else?

Chapter 13

Accelerating Change through Innovation

> The future is already here – it's just not evenly distributed.
>
> **– William Gibson**

Intrapreneurship and Entrepreneurship

Innovation will challenge the capacity of EHR governance processes in the coming years as intrapreneurs and entrepreneurs work fervently to transform the aesthetics, usability, and functionality of the EHR. Intrapreneurs will be disrupting themselves from within their own organizations, while entrepreneurs will be launching or refining business models that disrupt from outside. This will happen at a quick pace in a 4,000-year-old industry (healthcare) that often suffers from inertia while being highly reliant upon innovative technology. What to adopt (what not to adopt!), how to adopt it, and how to ensure end-user utility are all questions that will require EHR governance processes, at least in part.

Let's begin by understanding the customer. In 2021, there were an estimated 350,000 digital apps in healthcare competing for your attention, with more than 90,000 new ones introduced in 2020 alone.[1] They included tools for sleeping, eating, meditating, food shopping, and fitness classes; they can monitor blood pressure, heart rate, blood sugar and also do spirometry and capture an electrocardiogram. Internally many organizations, especially larger ones, have teams of data scientists and digital innovators spinning up new interfaces and dashboards to address pressing issues such as sepsis,

DOI: 10.4324/9781003008408-16

readmissions, perinatal mortality, and more. Without some coordination it is easy for these well-intentioned efforts to conflict with one another, or worse yet, become a distraction that offers little, if any, clinical value.

A good rule of thumb is that unless an app presents a complete solution, it is just noise. Solutions need to be comprehensive either by themselves or in seamless alignment with other technology. And they must be inclusive of clinician responsibilities and system workflows. Dr. Prentice Tom, Chief Medical Officer at Kintsugi, made this point clear with the following example.

Think about how you fry an egg. You grab a frying pan from the cabinet and place it on the stove top with a little butter or oil. You turn the heat on and let it warm up before cracking an egg or two into the pan. Maybe you sprinkle a little salt and pepper on your egg; some folks put a cover on the pan and others don't. A minute or so later you turn off the heat, slide the egg out of the pan onto a plate and off you go. Now what if I bring you the perfect pan for frying an egg (Figure 13.1). This pan makes an aesthetically pleasing, perfectly shaped fried egg every time and allows you to cook up to three eggs concurrently. Surely this will revolutionize the way you fry eggs. But months later we find our nifty little egg frying pan collecting dust in the back of the kitchen cupboard with the labels still attached simply because it doesn't support usual kitchen workflows.

Figure 13.1   **The ultimate pan for frying an egg.**

Restated another way by Dr. Robert Wachter, Chair of Medicine at UCSF,

> What we need to do is build not just the digital tools but also the workflow and processes. If patients are using a tool to manage their diabetes, there has to be a health system on the other side to make sure they get the care they need if they are not doing well.

As discussed in the previous chapter, the coordination of people, process, and technology is a key value of robust EHR governance. If something impacts the EHR (and associated workflows), it should be vetted through governance processes to minimize redundancies, coordinate complementary efforts, ensure technical feasibility, and allocate the build resources required for operationalization. This can only happen when each project, new software, API, or app has a change request or a series of linked change requests associated to it.

For example, I worked with one organization where the CMO sponsored the Chief Data Officer and his team to create a new care pathway for sepsis. The opportunity was huge with more than 1.5 million hospitalizations for sepsis each year with 30% of those cases resulting in death. Presenting signs and symptoms of sepsis are often subtle, so diagnosis and treatment could be delayed. The goal here was to leverage technology to develop a pathway to accelerate evidence-based best practice for the earlier detection of sepsis, improve outcomes, and decrease resource utilization. This involved the development and coordination of a sepsis app, a multi-phasic order set, a sepsis scorecard, and a sepsis dashboard.

I was invited to consult on this project and tasked with collaborating on EHR change request processes and governance group engagement. Coordinating all the pieces of this project and the resulting care pathway had its challenges. The dashboard needed to be interfaced through a URL into the EHR. The multi-phasic order set needed to be built, tested, socialized, and deployed (Figure 13.2). This required special attention as using multi-phasic order sets was a new workflow for many physicians. A dedicated clinical informatics resource collaborated with the sepsis project team to help deploy this project, educating physicians and nurses on the new

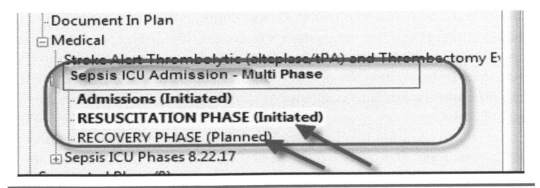

Figure 13.2 Deploying an order set with multiple phases to support a new sepsis care pathway with several integrated components.

order sets and workflow while ensuring the timely retirement of the older sepsis order sets.

As your organization innovates and adopts new technologies that impact your EHR and user experience, governance resources will be called upon to partner. Well-defined processes for conducting pilots, silent-mode testing, and proofs-of-concept should be some of the tools in your toolkit used to mitigate the people and process issues that arise when adopting new functionality. One day, when writing information from an external source back into the EHR becomes possible based on standards (*ONC interoperability rules, based on FHIR resources*), accelerated innovation will happen via app overlays onto the system. This will make the existing EHR a foundational operating system of sorts while expanding the scope and complexity of governance processes. Collaborate with your innovators by sharing risk and creating value.

Design Thinking

Design thinking is considered by many to be the holy grail of innovation — a concept made famous for solving wicked problems through a process of rapid-cycle iteration focused on user experience. John E. Arnold, Professor of Mechanical Engineering at Stanford University, first established the four areas of design thinking in 1959 in his text *Creative Engineering*.[2] With the rise of human-centered design in the 1980s and the formation of global design consultancy IDEO in the 1990s, design thinking became better known. In 2005, the Hasso Plattner Institute of Design at Stanford University began teaching design thinking as an approach to technical and social innovation. Then, in 2008, IDEO CEO Tim Brown published a seminal article in the *Harvard Business Review* defining the key characteristics of a design thinker and sharing examples of design thinking applied to (among other things) problem-solving in healthcare.[3] Today, in a world more interconnected and complex, the design thinking process of reframing problems through a user-centric lens continues to spawn innovation and out-of-the-box solutions.

The design thinking methodology has five stages – empathize, define, ideate, prototype, and test – which are depicted in a linear fashion but are intended to be fluid and flexible.

Stage 1: Empathize

The empathize phase is focused on understanding the problem you are trying to solve by getting to know the user. What do they want? What do they need? What are their objectives? This means observing, engaging, and listening to understand on a psychological and emotional level. To do this effectively, the designer must set aside preconceived notions and biases. Empathy is crucial. Leaders who may be inclined to solution jump are often tempted to bypass or abbreviate this phase. That would be a mistake since the information collected here is key to defining the success of the solution.

Stage 2: Define – State Your Users' Needs and Problems

Stage 2 is clearly articulating the problem in a user-centered way that identifies the population and the outcome. Simply stated, create a problem statement. This often sounds easier to do than it is. Yet the time spent in this phase sets the stage for success in the next. Remember, the only question a computer can answer is the one that you ask it.

Stage 3: Ideate – Challenge Assumptions and Create Ideas

Now, you're ready to generate ideas. The solid background of knowledge from the first two stages means you can start to *think outside-the-box*, look for alternative ways to view the problem, and identify innovative solutions to the problem statement you've created. Brainstorming is particularly useful here. When possible, invite outsiders and subject matter experts with different perspectives. Toward the end of this phase, you will narrow down to a few options to move forward with.

Stage 4: Prototype – Start to Create Solutions

Prototyping, stage 4, is about experimenting and turning ideas into tangible (although at times crude) products. The goal here is to do an initial round of testing to reveal constraints and flaws. Prototypes can be accepted, improved, redesigned, or rejected outright.

Stage 5: Test – Try Your Solutions Out

Testing which, due to resource constraints, is best done for high-value, high-risk options. A quick 2 × 2 table of risk and perceived value makes easier the task of identifying which solution(s) to test.

	High Perceived Value	*Low Perceived Value*
High Risk	Test	Throw It Out
Low Risk	Build It	Don't Test/Don't Build

Rigorously test the prototypes. Although this is the final stage, remember that design thinking is iterative and so the results from this stage may be used to redefine one or more additional problems.

In Chapter 2, we touched upon uTrace™, a mobile platform available on iOS and Android devices that allowed end users to track an EHR change request through its governance lifecycle (Figure 13.3). This app was developed with the collaboration of two teams, informatics and digital innovation, applying this design thinking framework to address end-user complaints about poor change request transparency. uTrace™ features included:

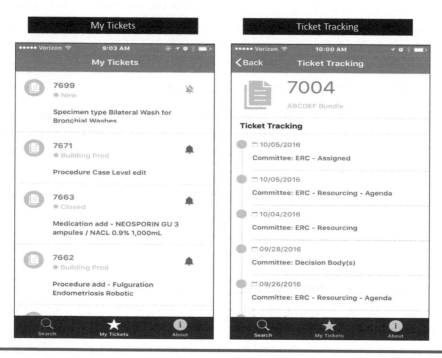

Figure 13.3   uTrace™, a mobile platform available on iOS and Android devices that allowed end users to track an EHR change request through its governance lifecycle.

- The ability to store and review recently viewed governance tickets.
- Search and advanced search features by clinical group, user, requesting region, and others.
- The ability to capture and store favorites to keep tabs on the most important tickets.
- Notifications to your device as a change request ticket of interest moves through the governance process.

■ A message center to review important notifications regarding your
ticket(s).

Simplify™ was a second mobile platform available on iOS and Android
devices that allowed physician end users to submit change requests quickly
without calling the help desk. This was developed in response to multiple end user complaints regarding bad help desk experiences. Simplify™
allowed users to:

■ Log help desk tickets and get status alerts right from their mobile
device.
■ Skim a newsfeed that was personalized to their specialty.
■ Watch select CME events to absorb knowledge anywhere.

One final place where we commonly see these design thinking concepts
applied in many EHR governance processes is through physician builder
or physician architect programs. About a decade ago, the larger EHR vendors began offering courses to teach, and eventually certify, physicians to
make changes within their EHR. Their logic, based in design thinking, was
simple – who better than a fellow physician could empathize, frame, and
understand the problem(s) being expressed by a colleague? These physician
architects can create and modify documentation templates used by their colleagues, build and adjust order sets, and some are even given the security to
work on clinical decision support tools, reports and dashboards. The value
in having these expensive resources in this role is that a physician often
understands the need faster and more thoroughly than an analyst, thereby
creating the best content in the least amount of time. Further, physicians can
often interpret what other clinicians are hoping to achieve by quickly reading between the lines. So often, a physician asks for tool *A*, but what they
really need is tool *B*. A physician builder can give the requestor what they
need, not what they want or asked for.

Data from the KLAS Arch Collaborative suggests that doctors who had a
physician builder or physician architect in their specialty were statistically
more satisfied with their EHR than doctors who didn't. While the reason
for this remains unclear, it may have nothing to do with their technical
build or architect skills. Physicians who understand how their EHR functions under the hood are exceptionally good at framing complicated technology issues in a way that their colleagues can understand. When an
irritable doctor wants to know why their EHR can't just do this or that, a

physician well-versed in the tool and familiar with organizational priorities can often strike the right note and convey information with candor, transparency and trust.

The application of design thinking in health information technology and innovation has the attention of several large healthcare systems around the country. Institutions such as Stanford,[4] Harvard, and Arizona State University all have biodesign labs while Apple Health partnered with 39 health systems to launch Apple Health Records; Google Health received attention for its partnership with Ascension Health; and Amazon has a partnership with EHR vendor, Cerner. Even the Centers for Medicare & Medicaid (CMS) has its own innovation center focused on testing various payment and service delivery models aimed at achieving better care for patients, smarter spending, and healthier communities.[5]

Never Waste a Good Crisis

The COVID-19 pandemic has been a stress test of EHR governance processes' ability to be nimble and responsive. Hospitals and medical groups alike have been challenged to rapidly launch or expand telehealth capabilities; capture, transmit, and receive patient data quickly; deliver and track vaccine public health efforts; implement evolving social distancing and isolation rules; seamlessly modify orders, order sets, and CDS rules; update formularies and diagnosis codes overnight; add new triage stations and external lab integration; and more. All this change has resurfaced the many harsh realities around fragmented health information, making interoperability of health data paramount. Data today is still locked down in individual EHR systems after each patient visit, and the flow of information to public health surveillance systems is antiquated often requiring paper and faxes. This lack of connectedness leads to duplicative tests, unnecessary care, and higher expenses.

As we discussed in the last chapter, new rules regarding interoperability standards and information blocking came at the time when we needed them most. They required the adoption of standards, specifically Fast Health Interoperability Resources (FHIR®) Version 4, to streamline the exchange of health data by providing a vendor-neutral API standard. Further, the ONC rule proposed the adoption of the US Core Data for Interoperability (USCDI) – a core set of data elements required to support nationwide interoperability. These rules in the wake of a global pandemic served as a forceful shove forward for interoperability. With new variants of the coronavirus currently igniting new surges of COVID-19 around the world, the need for data sharing through interoperability grows even more urgent. From understanding any single patient's complete medical journey to analyzing aggregated data at the community level, frontline providers and researchers need access to the most complete data sets available to track the disease, understand which protocols are most effective, and get out ahead of the virus.

Another area receiving a great deal of attention because of this crisis is telehealth. Who could have imagined that it would take 27 years and a global pandemic for telehealth to go mainstream? Over the course of the COVID-19 pandemic, EHR telehealth has grown from a $3 billion to a $250 billion industry, a game-changing event for physicians and patients alike. Experts agree that telehealth is here to stay, but the question on everyone's minds is who will deliver these services and how?

Early in the pandemic, providers – and CMS – justifiably had an *anything goes* approach to the technology platforms permissible for telehealth services. We soon learned, however, not all EHR telehealth functionalities are created equal. Some EHR-compatible telehealth tools add to organizational complexity by making data hard to access, being poorly customizable, or coming with a steep learning curve. It's one thing to say an EHR has telehealth capabilities, but it's important to evaluate whether the EHR integration is flexible enough to offer a user-friendly experience for both the physician and the patient.

It's also important to point out that virtual meeting solutions developed for businesses, while fine as a stop-gap solution, aren't a good way to deliver telehealth over the long term. The basic versions of these services are not HIPAA compliant, and information still needs to be entered into the EHR after the visit ends, which is time and labor intensive. The ideal telehealth experience should be like a virtual visit in the office, not the equivalent of Face Timing with a family member. The software should be embedded within the EHR system allowing an integrated experience from the time the patient shows up in the waiting room until the physician signs her note and orders. This decreases the cognitive and clinical burden of the process.

As telehealth continues to mature, providers will expect features such as video embedded within the EHR, integrated coding and billing, and a strong focus on patient experience. Certain factors such as improving the digital patient experience, the level of caregiver satisfaction, and strong customer support will drive competition in the current telehealth market and lead to substantial consolidation, likely reducing the current 260 vendors down to the 10–20 most mature vendors. From an EHR governance perspective, this may mean migrating to a new telehealth platform and additional build. Workflows and smart logic triggers (e.g., CDS) should also be evaluated since telehealth interfaces, information intake, and processes are often quite different. One system that evaluated this found 10 of their top 40 CDS rules were not being triggered appropriately during telehealth visits. This has profound implications for patient safety and patient care.

Chapter Summary

- Increasing amounts of innovation from intrapreneurs and entrepreneurs will challenge EHR governance processes to be nimble and responsive.
- In 2021, there were an estimated 350,000 digital apps in healthcare competing for your attention, with more than 90,000 new ones introduced in 2020 alone. Unless an app provides a complete solution, it is just noise.
- Engaging early with projects that will touch the EHR eases the burden on the project team and allows them to work within the construct of the governance processes to achieve the best possible design with the least amount of delay.
- The design thinking process of reframing problems through a user-centric lens has five stages:
  - Empathize
  - Define
  - Ideate
  - Prototype
  - Test
- Physician builder or physician architect programs allow design thinking concepts to be applied to EHR governance processes.
- The COVID-19 pandemic has been a stress test of EHR governance processes.
- Issues with interoperability received a push forward from regulations released in March 2020 promoting new standards in support of nation-wide interoperability.
- The COVID-19 pandemic has led to a boom in telehealth services that will require maturation, consolidation, and integration.

Chapter Exercises

1. Well-defined processes for conducting pilots, silent-mode testing, and proofs-of-concept should be some of the tools used to mitigate the people and process issues that arise when adopting new EHR functionality. Place a holder in your EHR Governance Toolkit and leverage real-use cases to develop documentation around these processes. You may get a jump start by checking in with other groups in your organization (EBM team, data science team) who may use these tools.

2. If you don't already have one, consider a physician builder or physician architect program at your hospital or health system. The benefits of a peer designer are significant and the costs are minimal. Your EHR vendor likely has resources explaining how it works and will have references to peer institutions so you can get first-hand insights.

Chapter 14

It's a Journey Not a Destination

It is better to travel well than to arrive.

– Buddha

Order Set Management

We've shared examples of how cross-team collaborations can expand the scope and value of your EHR governance processes. However, a mature governance framework can (and should) be leveraged to handle other functions, when able. For example, I've had physician governance groups take on the responsibility of regularly reviewing electronic order sets to assure alignment with evidence-based best practice. In one organization I worked with, we called this Evidence-based Knowledge Governance (EKG).

EKG focused exclusively on *existing* order sets, distinguishing it from requests for new order sets which proceeded through the change request process described earlier. To define the process and scope of EKG we needed to answer a few questions:

1. What order sets needed to be reviewed and how often?
2. Who was responsible for conducting the reviews?
3. What was the source of truth for determining best practice?
4. Would an order set management software (e.g., Zynx, Provation, something else) be used?
5. How would build between different domains be standardized and maintained?

DOI: 10.4324/9781003008408-17

6. How much additional resourcing would be required for EKG changes and where would it come from?
7. What would the review process look like?
8. How would changes be tracked over time (e.g., versioning)?
9. How would the effective and efficient use of physician time be ensured?

Several regulatory agencies endorse the *regular* review of order sets with many organizations requiring review every two to three years. The scope of EKG included any set of orders that required a licensed physician's or licensed medical provider's signature. Nursing-initiated orders, also commonly known as standing orders or protocols, and nursing plans of care were out of scope (Figure 14.1). Outside of this routine review cycle, updates to the literature around safety, quality, and best practice could also trigger a more frequent, ad hoc review.

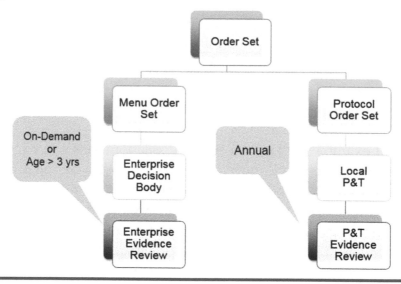

Figure 14.1   The scope of regular order set reviews was limited to those requiring a licensed physician's or licensed medical provider's signature (left). Nursing-initiated orders, also commonly known as standing orders or protocols, and nursing plans of care were out of scope (right).

EKG processes stipulated that order set reviews reflect a group majority consensus of subject matter experts and have their basis in evidence-based guidelines from well-respected agencies. This reflected the classic model of evidence-based medicine defined by David Sackett and colleagues.[1] Reviews were conducted in consultation with nursing, pharmacy, lab, the build team, and any other service appropriate to the order set under consideration. The EKG process can be summarized, at a high level, in eight steps:

1. Initiate an order set review based on the need for a routine update or some change to the best practice standard.
2. Edit the order set within a text document using the established mock-up guidelines.
3. Open an EHR governance change request ticket.
4. Bring the changes proposed to the physician decision body for review, refinement, and vote.
5. Update the change request with the voting approval date and finalized mock up document of changes.
6. Submit the change request to the gatekeeper body (e.g., routing) who will ensure it is complete before passing it through to resourcing to build.
7. Test in non-production and production environments.
8. Create a change communication to accompany the update release in the live environment.

Document Review

A custom code set was created within our EHR to track the date an order set was last reviewed as well as the group responsible for keeping it updated. This information, together with several existing data fields from the EHR, was exported into a business intelligence and data visualization software to create an EKG dashboard. The dashboard was interactive, allowing the application of a variety of filters including time, location, order set name, etc. By far, the most frequent function accessed was the one showing usage frequency within the last year by location and specialty (Figure 14.2).

Every month, each physician governance group responsible for performing EKG automatically received an Excel spreadsheet on their SharePoint site that listed the order sets under their review with usage and date last reviewed. Spreadsheet review was a standing agenda item in each month's meeting, allowing the voting members to rank the order of what to review next while keeping them appraised of what was in their queue (Figure 14.3). Once an order set was identified for EKG, it was assigned a physician and an informaticist to jointly perform the first level of review. This responsibility was rotated in a round robin fashion to be balanced and equitable. This first-level review dyad was responsible for bringing forth recommendations to the full governance body group for review and sign-off in a timely fashion.

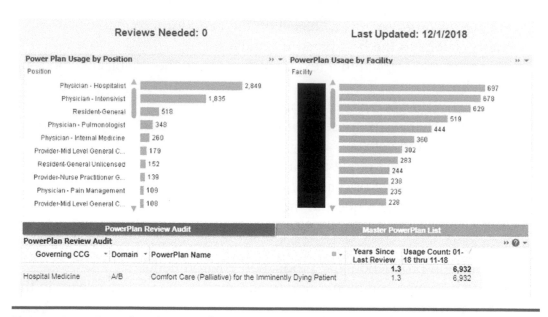

Figure 14.2   One view in an order set review dashboard used to track the primary physician group responsible for conducting the reviews, review status, and order set usage.

PowerPlan Review Audit					
Governing CCG		PowerPlan Name	Date Last Reviewed	Years Since Last Review	Usage Last 12 Months
Cardiology		Renal Clearance	10/01/2011	6.0	2,678
Cardiology	-	Postprocedure Pacemaker/Defibrillator Placement	02/01/2012	5.7	2,551
Cardiology	-	Coronary CTA (Cardiac)	03/01/2013	4.6	514
Cardiology	-	Amiodarone Orders for new onset Atrial Fibrillation	11/01/2013	3.9	1,828
Cardiology	-	Postprocedure: Diagnostic Cath/EP/IR (Red)	11/01/2013	3.9	11,206
Cardiology		PreProcedure/Acute Coronary Syn (ACS),Diagnostic/Intervention Cardiology (EP,Pacer,ICD,Cath)(Red)	11/01/2013	3.9	9,372
Cardiology		PreProcedure/Acute Coronary Syn (ACS),Diagnostic/Intervention Cardiology (EP,Pacer,ICD,Cath)(Red))	11/01/2013	3.9	4,592
Cardiology	-	Postprocedure Percutaneous Coronary Intervention (PCI AMI STEMI ACS)	12/01/2013	3.8	2,231
Cardiology	-	Heparin Infusion for ACS/Vascular (aPTT)	05/01/2014	3.4	2,241
Cardiology	-	Pre-op Elective Visit, Cardiac Surgery	03/01/2015	2.6	1,199
Cardiology	-	Postprocedure: Atrial Fibrillation Ablation	07/01/2015	2.3	867
Cardiology		Heparin Infusion for ACS/Vascular (Xa)	08/01/2015	2.2	407
Cardiology		Impella Bivalirudin Continuous Infusion Orders (HIT Only)	09/01/2015	2.1	9

Figure 14.3   An example of an order set review spreadsheet for the cardiology governance group. Order sets listed in red required routine review.

First-Level Review

The order set identified for review was pulled from the system in a rich text format making it easy to annotate. A simple but standardized system of color highlighting, developed in collaboration with our build team, was used to mock up the document with the requested changes. A green highlight indicates something should be *added*, a light blue highlight indicates that something should be *removed*, and a yellow highlight indicates the need to *change*

Unique Plan Description: Comfort Care (Palliative) for the Imminently Dying Patient
ADD
REMOVE
CHANGE

Comfort Care (Palliative) for the Imminently Dying Patient
ADT/Consents

Uncheck Patient Placement and POA

☐　Patient Placement
　　CMS has defined certain conditions that should never happen in the inpatient setting. Therefore if these
　　conditions are present on admission they should be appropriately documented in the order below.(NOTE)*
☐　Present on Admission
Code Status
☑　Do Not Resuscitate
☑　Goals of Care are Comfort Measures
Vital Signs
☑　Nursing Communication
　　　　Vital Signs Not necessary, do not wake, this supercedes other vital sign orders or protocols
☑　Vital Signs
　　　　Respiratory Rate and Heart Rate every 1 to 4 hours and as needed to assess comfort or dyspnea.
Activity
☐　Activity as Tolerated
　　　　Position patient for comfort PRN
☐　Bedrest
Patient Care
☑　Perineal Care
　　　　May order Foley catheter PRN discomfort

Note: This prechecked **EV Skin and Wound Care Protocol** order does <u>not</u> exist ▇▇▇

☑　EV Skin and Wound Care Protocol

Note: This *PRN for discomfort* order ▇ ▇▇reads **PRN for Comfort, End of Life care - existing Foley** ▇▇▇▇

☐　Insert Foley Catheter
　　　　PRN for Comfort, End of Life care - existing Foley
☐　Initate Standardized Procedure for RN Death Pronouncement
☑　Nursing Communication
　　　　Please communicate to Respiratory Therapy when family is ready for patient to be extubated.

Figure 14.4　**An example order set annotated as part of a routine order set review process. A green highlight indicates that something should be added, a light blue highlight indicates that something should be removed, and a yellow highlight indicates the need to change something.**

something. Some reviews generated a wide variety of changes (Figure 14.4) while others elicited none. Occasionally, an order set was retired in response to an EKG review and sometimes there was a realization that a net new order set was needed.

Opening a Change Request

Once an EKG review was underway, the informaticist engaged in the first-level review was responsible for placing a change request. This generated a ticket number that could be tracked through any decision-body meeting agenda as well as data on how long the EKG process was taking. All changes requested to a single order set had to be grouped together into a single change request ticket with the required supporting documentation attached. A ticket submission was not considered complete and would not be accepted for submission without the following information:

- A clear voting statement
- Assigned tester(s)
- Contact person for any build clarifications
- Presenter to committees/approval bodies

Decision Body Sign-Off

The first-level EKG review physician-informaticist dyad was responsible for bringing their recommendations to the larger governance decision-body group for consensus, review, and sign-off. This was intended to be a collegial and engaging process with the following ground rules:

- Speak candidly.
- Participate fully.
- Start and stop on time.
- Turn off cell phones/pagers or put on vibrate.
- Only one conversation at a time.
- Maintain confidentiality.
- Speak with one voice outside of the meeting and support consensus decisions.

Once the decision body approved the changes (with or without refinement), the informaticist updated the change request ticket and the governance processes unfolded as usual. There are three key principles to keep in mind when it comes to EKG:

- Changes reflect the group majority consensus
- Whenever possible, changes have their basis in evidence-based guidelines from a well-respected agency
- Reviews are conducted in consultation with nursing, pharmacy, lab, the build team, and any other services appropriate to the order set under consideration

Lessons Learned

If you want to embark on an EKG-like process, start small. Try unfolding and refining the process with one or two physician specialty groups that have a history of being risk tolerant and quick to provide thoughtful feedback. This initial pilot or proof-of-concept will get the wrinkles out of the process and make easier work of engaging more groups in the process. In fact, don't be surprised if, after you get your EKG process up-and-running, physician specialty groups approach you about participating.

Assigning an order set a clinical home can be tricky. Our first thought was that the group that used it the most should be responsible for maintaining best practice alignment. But our thinking changed as we realized, for example, that many of the cardiology order sets were used more by hospitalists or intensivists. We also saw a number of procedural order sets used frequently by Emergency Medicine physicians although we learned they were more appropriately maintained by other specialty groups.

Pharmacy and nursing are two key clinical partners to engage in EKG. Formulary standardization, therapeutic substitutions, and Antimicrobial Stewardship are just a few of the things, from a pharmacy perspective, that will impact order sets on a regular basis. And the potential impact of routine order set updates, protocols, and communication orders on nursing policy and workflows are self-evident.

Finally, maintain a tight alignment with your builders. They are the secret sauce to creating an annotation process that works, as well as connecting the dots after the voting is done to ensure a seamless build and deployment.

Legal and Ethical Considerations

Legal and compliance issues came up in our routing and governance meetings on a semi-regular basis. Compliance was a strong partner with EHR governance processes, attending routing meetings most weeks to keep abreast of what change requests were being made and what questions were being asked. Legal was available for consultation, as needed. It's important to be sensitive to these matters and to seek advice proactively.

Since EHRs went mainstream with the passage of the HITECH Act in 2019, malpractice providers have been tracking the number and causes of EHR-related claims. In a 2019 analysis spanning 10 years, Coverys[2] found documentation accounted for 72% of all EHR-related risk issues, including users looking at the wrong dropdown, the wrong screen, out-of-date information, or documenting on the wrong chart. Diagnosis-related allegations comprised both the highest percentage of events as well as the highest indemnity payments in EHR events. Other issues included confusing system design and incorrect patient information due to a system conversion as well as general EHR usability. Doctors Company,[3] in a similar analysis spanning 2010–2018, found that EHRs were typically a contributing factor rather than the primary cause of malpractice claims. The frequency of these claims overall was low, although the pace grew from a low of seven cases in 2010 to an average of 22.5 cases per year in 2017 and 2018. They offered their physicians several suggestions including (1) avoid copying and pasting except when describing the patient's past medical history, (2) contact the IT department if the auto-populate feature in their EHR was causing erroneous data to be recorded, and (3) review entries after making a choice from a dropdown menu to make sure the intended choice was captured. Constellation,[4] in an analysis spanning 2010–2014, demonstrated that 63% of the identified EHR issues were user-related and 58% were tech-related. User issues included miscellaneous errors, hybrid record/conversion issues, incorrect information, and pre-populating or copy and paste of information. The most prevalent tech issue was system and software design, followed by the routing of electronic data and system dysfunction or malfunction.

In response to these evolving EHR-related medico-legal issues, the ONC started creating SAFER guides.[5] Today there are nine SAFER guides which are organized into three broad domains: *safe health IT* (45 total recommendations); *using health IT safely* (80 total recommendations); and *monitoring health IT* (15 total recommendations). Each guide is a checklist-based self-assessment tool designed to improve the safety of how the EHR is used. CMS recently required all organizations to attest to completing these SAFER guides on an annual basis.

Robust, responsive, end-user-driven EHR governance will continue to be a crucial tool for recognizing and mitigating many of the identified risks of EHR use. These governance processes, when driven by the voice of the customer, identify potential problems early, acting in some ways like a surveillance system. Early recognition allows for quicker resolution, and ideally prevention.

Larry Ozeran, President of Clinical Informatics Inc., asked me if this book had a section on ethics. He went on to explain,

> every time we make a choice there is an ethical component. Few people appreciate how subliminal those ethical dilemmas are and as a result they never explicitly discuss them. Leadership assumes everyone is ethical, but not in any specific or, perhaps more importantly, consistent way. Do you talk about how to manage situations when the principles might conflict? Do you rank the principles? Is human life explicitly more important in making implementation decisions than cost, or is human life more of a nice-to-have?

I pondered those questions and wondered whether the core values estab-lished for an EHR governance process (e.g., voice, choice, fair, equitable, transparent and accountable) provided an ethical compass (Figure 14.5).

Governance Core Values

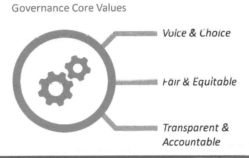

Voice & Choice

Fair & Equitable

Transparent & Accountable

Figure 14.5 **Core values identified for EHR governance in a large healthcare system.**

Dr. Ozeran acknowledged that those were the first step in identifying gov-ernance priorities, but not a replacement for a focused ethics discussion. He warned:

> you actually consider choices differently when you have explic-itly discussed your ethics and your ethical obligations. When they are unstated, you have less moral accountability and it is easier to make ethical compromises because you and your team haven't openly agreed to follow any particular ethical path.

Captured by his perspective, I dove deeper to find a body of literature on ethics and informatics. While a full-blown discussion of the subject is beyond the scope of this book, there are several ethical issues unique to the EHR worth mentioning. The ethics involved with EHR governance extend from the five foundational principles of autonomy (the right of self-determination), beneficence (advancing the good of others), non-maleficence (preventing harm), integrity (performing to the best of one's ability) and the principle of impossibility (working within the confines of what is possible). Part of this uniqueness is centered on the special relationship between the EHR and the subject of that record. The EHR not only reveals much about the patient that is private and should be kept confidential but, more impor-tantly, it functions as the basis of decisions that have a profound impact on the welfare of the patient. The patient is in a vulnerable position, and any decision regarding the patient and the EHR must acknowledge the fun-damental necessity of striking an appropriate balance between ethically justified ends and otherwise appropriate means. Further, the data that is contained in the EHR also provides the raw materials for decision-making by healthcare institutions, governments and other agencies without which a system of healthcare delivery simply could not function. EHR governance, through its roles in overseeing the design, build, maintenance, storage, access, use, and manipulation of the EHR, has a voice in this conversation. We'll explore this further in an exercise at the end of this chapter.

Land and Expand

Since the turn of the century, well over 1000 healthcare organizations have gone through either a merger or an acquisition to improve economies of scale and revenue synergies. In recent years, as healthcare has become increasingly digitized, these newly formed care delivery organizations have grappled with how to merge their IT infrastructures, interfaces and software. One key business decision facing leaders is whether to move to a single EHR or, when already on the same EHR, a single instance of that platform. There are obvious benefits to everyone being on the same version of the same software in terms of governance structures, maintenance and licensing costs, data integrity, and digital integration. Likewise, there are significant costs in terms of financing consolidation projects, potential productivity loss, the impact of the change on the people and their processes, and the loss of historical data in the new EHR. Holmgren and Adler-Milstein found that about half of healthcare systems had not aligned their EHR systems after a merger or acquisition, but in the 35% who did, it was usually with one of the two largest vendors, Epic or Cerner.[6] Dr. Brett Daniel, CMIO at Optum Washington, offers some wisdom from a fair amount of experience with this.

> Instance alignment can be defined as moving providers on one customized version of an EHR onto a different customized version of the same EHR. Think of it like migrating onto a new iPhone with different apps. It still looks and feels the same to some degree, but it is customized differently. Unfortunately, migrating patient data is not as simple as a download from the cloud on your new phone. In fact, data migration is much more complex and complicated. With four instance alignments under my belt, and a likely fifth in my future, here are four key lessons learned over the years.

1. <u>Same vendor does not mean the same EHR</u>

The good news is that most of the current users of an EHR will understand the basic features and usability of the newer version of the same vendor EHR. The bad news is that the users might be used to an outdated and customized version that has different workflows for high volume things like lab collection, billing for clinical procedures, or phases of care orders. What had been a routine workflow in the past, now results in lost orders, missing charges, and frustration with the new system. Additionally, for the first year after transition, most change requests or emails start with, *In our version of the EHR we could do this and it worked great, but this new version does not work that way. We want to bring back this previous workflow that we had.* Strong shared governance and reliable communication are important to mitigate these requests and concerns that are usually no longer possible in the new version.

When aligning instances of your EHR, there will also need to be some refinement to your training. Most of the users understand basic functions, so it is important to spend more time on personalization and translating key workflow differences from the previous version. Login labs are still important to make sure templates and accesses were transferred correctly. There can also be a sense of complacency in the staff about already knowing their version of the same EHR and not needing to attend training sessions. So, it is important to have a clear value equation on the time being requested for training.

2. <u>Data migration is the key driver of success</u>

There is no question that the success of these projects relies heavily upon a robust data migration strategy. Printer mappings will get fixed. Accesses will get rectified. The system will eventually feel more normal. However, the grind of having to reconcile data, rebuild the patient chart, hunt down scanned documents or bounce between the previous version and the new one for patient care is grueling for the first six plus months after instance alignment. Providers and staff do not have the time in their day to take on this additional burden easily. The more data that can be migrated electronically, the better. Build or use vendor interfaces for labs, imaging, notes, flowsheets, and history. Use chart abstractors for the first several weeks of procedures and office visits to reconcile patient information and remove the burden from the frontline care teams who are just trying to learn the system and get through their day. Besides the burden on your care teams to rebuild an accurate chart, data migration is also vital for rebuilding your quality infrastructure, risk capture tools, and the information in your patient portal. Data migration needs broad involvement from operations, HIM, informatics, providers, and should be a pillar in your project to drive success.

3. Cultural transformation and policy alignment

This is not an IT project. This is a transformation of the organizations into a shared clinical, governance, data, and operational model. There is a sense of loss for the organization being moved to the new version of their EHR. There are fears about loss of autonomy or being able to deliver the same care. It can be cumbersome to add more voices to making changes that will impact entire service lines now in both organizations. It is time consuming to modify all the policies that will be impacted when having to use the same build for things like nurse protocols, blood administration, or procedural sedation. Order set contents are another particular pain point. It is important to seek consensus around care pathways, policies, and standard procedures early on.

Like most organizational transformation, it is important to lead with vision of the benefits of coming together and using a shared medical record. Leaders across the organization need to agree on the importance and priority of this project. While IT and informatics play key roles in the technical aspects, operational and human resource leaders need to be heavily involved in leading the people and process changes.

4. Simplify applications and integrations

One benefit of aligning on one instance of an EHR is that it simplifies your infrastructure, reduces your overall costs, and builds a single foundation upon which to connect your digital continuum of care. Take this opportunity to further simplify your portfolio of third-party applications that interface into the EHR. It might also be an opportunity to update some of those on-prem biomedical devices into more modernized network solutions. While rationalizing your application portfolio adds additional complexity, it also affords the opportunity to recognize contractual savings, simpler data flows, and reduced maintenance costs.

To summarize, EHR instance alignment is a complex cultural and technological transformation for a healthcare organization. Simplifying your core systems of patient care has clear advantages as we evolve systems of intelligence and patient engagement to integrate with that core in our evolving patient care continuum. While moving onto the same EHR vendor sounds like it would simplify the process, the truth is that many of the same challenges remain with workflow changes, data migration, policy alignment, governance models, and third-party applications.

Another common scenario is migrating providers from one mature EHR onto another mature version of a *different* EHR. A memorable example of this was with an oncology group within a large healthcare system that I worked with. For several years there was only one hospital providing oncology services through our EHR's oncology module. An extensive work effort was required to bring them onto the platform but afterwards growth and optimization was driven by their own needs simply because they were the only ones in the organization using the functionality. Requests from this oncology group came through standard EHR governance processes to ensure completeness and technical feasibility, but decision-body consensus wasn't required prior to resourcing for build since the impact was limited to the one group. That changed in 2018 with the addition of a second hospital with outpatient clinics and infusion centers to the module.

There are many issues that need to be addressed when expanding an existing functionality to a new group, facility, or region. The initial group has often devoted much time and energy to defining build, demonstrating proof-of-concept, and is heavily invested in their processes and workflows. The longer they have been the only group using a functionality, the harder scaling can be. Playing well in the sandbox with others may not come easily. It was amid these growing pains that we expanded the use of this oncology module to the new group. When only one hospital was using the oncology module there was no need to obtain consensus and formally vet new regimen requests. Now with the addition of this second group (and the promise of additional groups in the future), a vetting and consensus process was needed. One place this was a particular pain point was the process of making new oncology regimens available in the EHR. Current state it took approximately 90 days to operationalize a new oncology regimen but with the addition of the second group, the request was made for a 2-week turnaround time (TAT).

There was consensus that the National Comprehensive Cancer Network (NCCN) was the best practice standard for oncology care but because their field evolved so rapidly, there could be up to a six-month lag time from when a new oncology regimen was reported in the medical literature to when NCCN formally adopted it as a best practice standard. This included newly approved drugs by the FDA as well as new indications and routes of administration for existing drugs. There was a need to be more agile since that was the standard of care most oncologists were trained to and the expectation that their patients had. There was awareness of a generic oncology regimen template within the EHR that could be customized as needed, but many oncologists and pharmacists saw it as a stop-gap measure in need of a permanent solution.

Armed with a clear understanding of the problem, we convened a small cross-disciplinary team to brainstorm. There was immediate agreement that any request for a new regimen needed to be translated into a governance change request (Figure 14.6). Since oncology regimens are a very structured

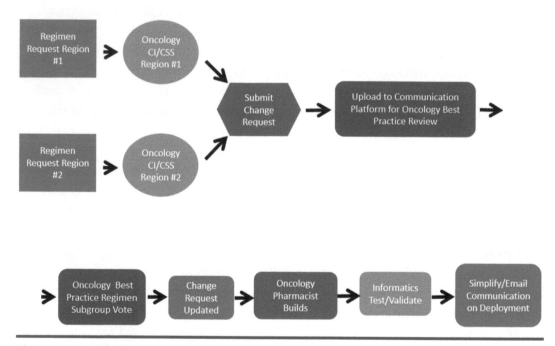

Figure 14.6 **The process established for requesting a new oncology regimen. A virtual communication platform was used to vet and approve requests rapidly and a dedicated resource ensured a quick build post-approval. The goal was to have this unfold, from start to finish, in two weeks.**

type of build, a template was created to assist the submitter in providing the required information. Submission of the change request into our change management software was accompanied by an email to our EHR governance inbox alerting a team member of a net new regimen request. It was at this point that the clock started to tick for measuring TAT.

The request was promptly posted into an oncology best practice group on our virtual communication platform (Chapter 10). The oncology physicians in this group were empowered to approve, refine, or disapprove the request. A 48-hour response time was requested. Once approved, the change request was updated and resourced to a dedicated oncology builder. Testing and validation were done by the informaticists supporting oncology in the two locations, and communication of deployment was done via a communications app and email.

This process was bold and pushed the limits of what our governance processes had been able to do. It required (among other things) a seamless partnership with our oncology best practice team, use of a virtual communication platform, new rule logic within our change request defect management system, a dedicated oncology build resource, and a new communication methodology. Progress was tracked in weekly project management meetings. Initial problems included securing the build resource and acclimating the oncology physicians to the communication platform. We knew there was a lot of change that needed to be embraced to reach the requested two-week TAT, so patience and persistence were abundant.

When I rolled off this project, many of the obstacles had been mitigated or overcome. Oncology regimen TAT was improving but had not yet achieved the targeted two-week goal. There was a keen awareness that the process was hitting turbulence and physicians who might otherwise be inclined to complain were more understanding of how challenging it was for a colleague to weigh in rapidly on best practice sign-off. In this way, EHR governance processes offered a continuous opportunity to collaborate in rapid cycle process improvement.

Another example where EHR governance processes were called to collaborate in an innovative fashion was when one organization started migrating outpatient providers onto the ambulatory module of the same EHR being used within their hospitals. *One Patient, One Chart* was the rallying call as the patient-facing benefits of having all care information in one place were socialized. The Family Medicine physician could now easily see what happened when the patient visited the Emergency Department over the weekend. The intensivist could see the POLST and advanced directives the primary care physician had placed on the chart. Lab results, radiology reports, and pharmacy information were no longer siloed in individual EHRs but were visible for all to see across the continuum of care. This treasure trove of shared information raised two important questions – who was responsible for maintaining what part of the chart and who had decision rights for making changes? This was a particularly sticky question when it came to specific workflows like managing the problem list or performing medication reconciliation. And what happened when a change request had both inpatient and ambulatory impact? Who got the final say in the matter?

As per the usual process with our EHR governance framework, the gatekeeper function (e.g., routing) determined which change requests required voting from ambulatory decision-making bodies. However, IT and EHR governance also partnered with ambulatory business leaders to develop a unified care delivery model that set priorities for new EHR functionality. A new group was created charged with developing and maintaining strategy and operational guidelines for the care delivery model across all ambulatory entities within the organization, including the technology used to support this model. This group had two subcommittees tasked with (1) reviewing and refining all ambulatory originating EHR governance tickets and (2) prioritizing and rank ordering ambulatory change requests. This two-prong approach to expanding the existing governance body framework and partnering with ambulatory business leaders to crosswalk the voice and choice of ambulatory providers lent clarity to questions of shared governance that came with using one EHR across the continuum of care. As the organization and EHR matured, this theme of partnering with the business on governance processes reoccurred. This organically shifted the EHR governance focus to outcome metrics with a broader, more transformative impact on care delivery. This marked a transition to EHR 3.0 that we discussed in Chapter 1 (Figure 14.7).

Figure 14.7   A representation of the evolution of EHR governance processes. It began with the initial adoption of the software (EHR 1.0), and then transitioned toward refinement and optimization (EHR 2.0), finally maturing into an agent of transformation driving outcomes (EHR 3.0).

The maturation that EHR governance processes experienced in moving to EHR 3.0 paralleled similar growth of the teams responsible for the *define* and *discover* work within the organization. A rapid increase in the number of clinical councils defining best practice provided a strong complement to an innovative data science team leveraging the resources of a data warehouse and data lake. These three groups (define, design and discover) worked together in an agile, iterative fashion, complimenting, pushing, and at times antagonizing each other (Figure 14.8). Having someone from each

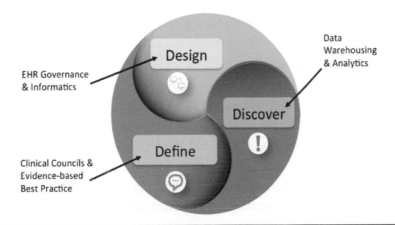

Figure 14.8   A cyclical and interdependent relationship between *defining* best practice, *designing* an elegant interface, and *discovering* insights (the three Ds) that form the balanced foundation required to sustain and support a learning healthcare system.

of the three D groups in most larger projects sponsored by the organization improved efficiencies by breaking down silos, decreasing confusion, setting realistic expectations and driving innovation. This joint focus on well-defined outcomes, over time, bore fruit and drove value in a learning healthcare system.

Chapter Summary

- A mature EHR governance framework can and should be leveraged to handle other related functions, when able.
- A process for handling the routine review of physician order sets is one example described in detail.
- Partner with legal and compliance as these types of issues come up routinely during the vetting of EHR change requests.
- Some of the more common EHR-related issues in malpractice claims include:
  - Documentation errors,
  - Diagnosis-related errors,
  - Errors due to maintaining hybrid systems,
  - Data migration or conversion errors,
  - Copy and paste or copy forward errors, and
  - Confusing system and software design.
- The core values you identified in Chapter 6, while a strong foundation for identifying EHR governance priorities, do not replace an explicit conversation about ethics.
- Scaling functionality or expanding scope can pose unique challenges for the early adopters who defined the initial build and workflows.
- Helping end users adjust to the expanding scope of an EHR poses unique challenges requiring patience and persistence.
- As EHR governance functions mature and partner with evolving define and discover functions, the learning healthcare system matures.

Chapter Exercises

1. Once you have a mature EHR governance framework (not before), consider what other functions it can drive. Routine order set management is a natural extension of EHR design work and the example presented within this chapter. Are there others? Don't forget to update your EHR Governance Toolkit or draft a separate charter for the new process(es) if that is more appropriate.

2. There are several tools and resources available for managing EHR risk. Take the time to review the SAFER guides referenced within the chapter (*https://www.healthit.gov/topic/safety/safer-guides*). There are currently nine of them organized into three broad domains: *safe health IT* (45 total recommendations); *using health IT safely* (80 total recommendations); and *monitoring health IT* (15 total recommendations). CMS mandates that all organizations attest to completing these SAFER guides on an annual basis.

   Other resources worth a look:
   - AHRQ Workflow Assessment Toolkit (*https://digital.ahrq.gov/health-it -tools-and-resources/evaluation-resources/workflow-assessment-health -it-toolkit*)
   - AHRQ's Guide to Reducing Unintended Consequences in the EHR (*https://digital.ahrq.gov/sites/default/files/docs/publication/guide-to -reducing-unintended-consequences-of-electronic-health-records.pdf*)
   - ECRI Partnership for Health IT Patient Safety (*https://www.ecri.org/ solutions/hit-partnership*)

3. Ethical mores for EHR governance are distinct from, but aligned with, core values. Take the time to explicitly define this with your guiding coalition. Use the information provided within this chapter to start the conversation. The more specific you are, the better adherence and accountability you will likely have.

Epilogue

Feeling overwhelmed?

I was too when I first started doing this work.

But you don't need to be.

Developing or optimizing EHR governance processes is a pleasurable journey if you simply remember one thing – it's a team sport. *It's a Team Sport!*

It takes time, vigilance, and patience, no matter where you are in your journey.

The burden when things go poorly (and the praise when things go well) doesn't belong to any one person.

Share the wins. Share the losses.

On days when it might be hard to see the light at the end of the tunnel, ask for help.

Live your core values.

Some things will need to be done and redone several times. Other things will work perfectly the first time.

But it's all worth it when a colleague thanks you for making something easier and a patient has a better healthcare experience.

That's why we do what we do.

And it's so rewarding.

Notes

Chapter 1

1. https://mcdac.blogspot.com/2008/12/president-elect-barack-obamas-december.html
2. Definition of Informatics from the American Medical Informatics Association (AMIA). https://amia.org/about-amia/why-informatics
3. Schulte F., Fry E. Death by 1,000 Clicks: Where Electronic Health Records Went Wrong. https://khn.org/news/death-by-a-thousand-clicks/
4. Wachter, Robert M. *The Digital Doctor: Hope, Hype, and Harm at the Dawn of Medicine's Computer Age.* New York: McGraw-Hill; 2015. ISBN: 9780071849463.
5. *Harvard Business Review*, How Physicians Can Keep Up with the Knowledge Explosion in Medicine. https://hbr.org/2016/12/how-physicians-can-keep-up-with-the-knowledge-explosion-in-medicine
6. IOM Report, Best Care at Lower Cost: The Path to Continuously Learning Health Care in America. http://www.nationalacademies.org/hmd/Reports/2012/Best-Care-at-Lower-Cost-The-Path-to-Continuously-Learning-Health-Care-in-America.aspx
7. Dean W., Talbot S. Physicians Aren't "Burning Out." They're Suffering from Moral Injury. STAT. Jul 26, 2018. [Accessed August 19, 2019]. https://www.statnews.com/2018/07/26/physicians-not-burning-out-they-are-suffering-moral-injury/
8. National Academy of Medicine, Taking Action against Clinician Burnout: A Systems Approach to Professional Well-Being. https://nam.edu/systems-approaches-to-improve-patient-care-by-supporting-clinician-well-being/
9. https://www.ashclinicalnews.org/spotlight/rethinking-burnout/
10. Writer, speaker, and physician advocate. https://www.nishamehtamd.com/
11. Arndt B.G., Beasley J.W., Watkinson M.D., et al. Tethered to the EHR: Primary Care Physician Workload Assessment Using EHR Event Log Data and Time-Motion Observations. *Ann Fam Med.* 2017;15:419–26.

12. Dean W., Talbot S. Physicians Aren't "Burning Out." They're Suffering from Moral Injury. STAT. Jul 26, 2018. [Accessed August 19, 2019]. https://www .statnews.com/2018/07/26/physicians-not-burning-out-they-are-suffering-moral -injury/

Chapter 2

1. https://ehrintelligence.com/news/himss-40-of-organizations-have-no-formal-ehr -governance/
2. https://klasresearch.com/arch-collaborative
3. Arch Collaborative "Pyramid of Change" case study https://klasresearch.com/ archcollaborative/casestudy/pyramid-of-change/2
4. https://www.destination-innovation.com/

Chapter 3

1. https://www.nap.edu/catalog/9728/to-err-is-human-building-a-safer-health -system
2. https://www.healthdatamanagement.com/list/the-10-largest-patient-safety -concerns-for-2019
3. https://www2.deloitte.com/content/dam/Deloitte/us/Documents/life-sciences -health-care/us-lshc-physician-survey-hit-factsheet.pdf
4. Sackett David L., Rosenberg William M.C., Gray J.A. Muir, Haynes R. Brian, Richardson W. Scott. Evidence based medicine: what it is and what it isn't, *BMJ* 1996; 312:71.
5. https://www.forbes.com/forbes-insights/our-work/c-suite-outlook/
6. Asq.org. 2016. *Plan-Do-Check-Act Cycle (PDCA Cycle) - ASQ*. [online] Available at: http://asq.org/learn-about-quality/project-planning-tools/overview/pdca -cycle.html
7. In his book *Leading Change*, John Kotter takes us on an 8 step journey on how to approach organizational transformation: (1) create urgency, (2) form a powerful coalition, (3) create a vision for change, (4) communicate the vision, (5) empower action, (6) create quick wins, (7) build on change and (8) make it stick.

Chapter 4

1. In his book *Start with Why*, Simon Sinek champions a model of thinking from the inside-out. Start with your purpose (why), next define your process (how) and finish with your results (what). Sinek argues our limbic brain first seeks to trust and understand (why, how) so that your neocortex can then analyze, rationalize, and respond.

2. My training as a medical epidemiologist and ASQ Lean Six Sigma Green Belt inclines me to weave this methodology into almost everything I do. DMAIC is, in my experience, an intuitive and comprehensive framework for problem-solving.
3. Kotter, John P. *Harvard Business Review*, To Create Healthy Urgency, Focus on a Big Opportunity, February 21, 2014. https://hbr.org/2014/02/to-create-healthy-urgency-focus-on-a-big-opportunity
4. Kotter, John P., *Harvard Business Review*, Four Ways to Increase the Urgency Needed for Change, April 15, 2009. https://hbr.org/2009/04/four-ways-to-increase-the-urge
5. Garrette B., Phelps C., and Sibony O. *Cracked It!: How to Solve Big Problems and Sell Solutions like Top Strategy Consultants.* Palgrave Macmillan; 2019. https://cracked-it-book.com
6. https://hbr.org/2017/01/are-you-solving-the-right-problems

Chapter 5

1. Auerbach A.D., Khanna R., Adler-Milstein J. Letting a Good Crisis Go to Waste. *J Gen Intern Med.* 2020;35(4):1289–1291. doi:10.1007/s11606-019-05552-z
2. Indira Sriram, Robin Harland, Steven R. Lowenstein. I, EHR. *J. Hosp. Med* 2020;2;119–120. Published online first May 10, 2019. doi:10.12788/jhm.3211
3. https://en.wikipedia.org/wiki/Na%C3%AFve_realism
4. Source: HFMA National Institute. https://www.hfma.org/
5. https://en.wikipedia.org/wiki/Reflective_listening
6. https://hbr.org/2001/10/harnessing-the-science-of-persuasion

Chapter 6

1. James C. Collins and Jerry I. Porras, Building Your Company's Vision, *Harvard Business Review*, September–October 1996
2. https://www.healthit.gov/topic/standards-technology/standards/fhir-fact-sheets

Chapter 7

1. https://www.thehedgescompany.com/books/
2. https://jeffreypfeffer.com/research-articles/
3. https://www.tesla.com/blog/all-our-patent-are-belong-you

Chapter 8

1. https://www.forbes.com/sites/aileron/2012/12/27/keeping-your-enemies-closer/#471410505727

Chapter 9

1. Campbell E.M., Sittig D.F., Ash J.S., et al. Types of Unintended Consequences Related to Computerized Provider Order Entry. *J Am Med Inform Assoc.* 2006 Sep–Oct; 13(5): 547–556.
2. https://en.wikipedia.org/wiki/Hype_cycle
3. https://www.whatmatters.com/

Chapter 10

1. Osheroff, J.A., Teich, J., Levick, D., Saldana, L., Velasco, F., Sittig, D., Rogers, K., & Jenders, R. (2012). Improving Outcomes with Clinical Decision Support: An Implementer's Guide, Second Edition (2nd ed.). HIMSS Publishing. https://doi .org/10.4324/9780367806125.

Chapter 11

1. https://hbr.org/2018/01/the-leaders-guide-to-corporate-culture
2. *Harvard Business Review*, December 31, 2018 *How to Embrace Change Using Emotional Intelligence.* https://hbr.org/2018/12/how-to-embrace-change-using -emotional-intelligence

Chapter 12

1. https://en.wikipedia.org/wiki/ITIL
2. https://www.itilnews.com/index.php?pagename=ITIL__Back_to_basics_People _Process_and_Technology#
3. https://www.christopherspenn.com/2018/01/transforming-people-process-and -technology-part-1/
4. https://klasresearch.com/
5. https://klasresearch.com/arch-collaborative
6. https://klasresearch.com/article/the-arch-collaborative-learning-center -knowledge-at-your-fingertips/809
7. Bersin by Deloitte, 2013 (Get full citation from WIT presentation)

Chapter 13

1. https://www.mobihealthnews.com/news/digital-health-apps-balloon-more -350000-available-market-according-iqvia-report
2. https://en.wikipedia.org/wiki/John_E._Arnold

3. https://readings.design/PDF/Tim%20Brown,%20Design%20Thinking.pdf
4. https://biodesign.stanford.edu/programs/fellowships/innovation-fellowships/program-curriculum.html
5. https://innovation.cms.gov/

Chapter 14

1. Richardson P.E., David Sackett and the Birth of Evidence Based Medicine: How to Practice and Teach EBM. *BMJ*. 2015 Jun 8;350:h3089. doi: 10.1136/bmj.h3089. PMID: 26055193.
2. https://www.coverys.com/
3. https://www.thedoctors.com/
4. https://constellationmutual.com/
5. https://www.healthit.gov/topic/safety/safer-guides
6. Holmgren A. and Adler-Milstein J. (2019, March 7). *Does Electronic Health Record Consolidation Follow Hospital Consolidation?* Health Affairs Blog. doi: 10.1377/hblog20190304.998205

Index

A

Accountability, 68, 74, 83–84, 93, 105, 121, 135, 155, 205, 215
AI-driven systems, 12
Alignment, 13, 34, 60, 63, 96, 111–112, 124, 159, 170–171, 186, 197, 203, 209
  instance, 206–208
Ambient voice technology, 171
Ambulatory, 74, 84–87, 131, 211–212
American healthcare system, 4
American Medical Informatics Association (AMIA), 4
Analyze step, 45
Anecdotal feedback, 108
Anger, 56, 161
Antimicrobial stewardship program, 35, 82, 203
Anxiety, 53, 55–56, 120, 158
  -based urgency, 55
Application programming interface (API), 99, 101, 187, 192
Aspirin, 11
Asynchronous, 42, 104, 146, 151, 179, 181–183
Atomic Energy Act, 54
Authority culture values, 158
Automation, 6, 12, 170, 182
  streamlines processes, 139–140
Autonomy, 7, 12–13, 15–16, 70–71, 78, 116, 161, 205, 208

B

Behavior, 69, 82, 111, 120, 154–156, 163
Big data, 37
Bottleneck, 27, 118
Bottom-up/end-user requests, 25, 27–28, 31, 38, 117
Brain scans, 110
Break/fix request, 24, 32, 88–89
Burden electronic documentation, 21, 72–73, 75, 130–131, 135
Burning platforms, 56
Burnout, 12–14, 16–17, 56, 120
Business case, 58–65, 87, 92, 108, 131, 133, 148–149
Bypass, 87–89

C

Caring culture values, 157
Carrot-and-stick approach, 5
Centers for Disease Control and Prevention (CDC), 5, 53
Centers for Medicare & Medicaid Services (CMS), 5, 8, 130, 192–193, 204, 215
Centralized requests, 25
Centralized vs. decentralized decision-making, 29
Change fatigue, 115, 119, 120, 125
Change management process, see Leading change model

Change requests, 6–8, 16, 20, 22, 24–25, 27–28, 31–32, 41–42, 49, 58–63, 82, 84–87, 91–93, 97, 101, 133, 135, 145, 147, 149, 178, 187, 191, 203, 207, 212, 214
  approvals tab, 61–62
  build and actions tabs, 62
  details tab, 60–61
  format in virtual platform, 148
  submissions, 89
  TAT, 133
  types, 88
Change tolerance, 119
Chief Health Information Officer, 72
Clinical decision support (CDS), 8–9, 11, 16, 35, 61, 108, 141–143, 191
  Healthcare organization
    active provider alerts, 143
    alert analytics, 144
    alerts fired, 144
  right channel, 11
  right format, 11
  right information, 10
  right person, 10
  rights of, 143
  right time in workflow, 11–12
  workflow process, 142
Clinical informaticist, 72, 87, 92, 128, 132, 180–181
Common Clinical Data Set (CCDS), 99
Communication, 13–14, 21, 26–27, 41, 49, 62–63, 69, 76–77, 89, 94, 103–114, 118, 133, 146–147, 149, 151, 154, 171, 177, 199, 203, 207, 210–211
  skills and traditions, 105–108
  tools, 104–105
Complexity scoring tool, 27, 31–32
Complex problem-solving, 57
Compliance, 28, 60, 73, 85, 91, 133, 158, 203, 214
Confusion, 161
Consensus-driven governance, 6, 68, 75, 84, 90, 101, 125, 176, 182
Consistency, 77
Control step, 45
Core ideology, 81–82, 102
Core purpose, 82

Core values, 69, 81–84, 101–102, 105, 113, 135, 155, 205, 215
  accountability, 68, 74, 83–84, 93, 105, 121, 135, 155, 205, 215
  choice, 7, 15, 67–68, 83, 205, 212
  equitability, 83, 205
  fairness, 83, 205
  transparency, 13, 43, 59, 68, 83, 121, 123, 133, 135, 154, 190, 192, 205
  voice, 6, 15, 67–68, 83, 205, 212
Coumadin, 11
COVID-19 pandemic, 192, 193
Credibility, 69
Culture, 6, 37, 43–45, 47, 68, 75, 82, 116, 120, 126, 135, 146, 153–165
  of change, 43
  norms, 155
  of safety, 13, 35, 68
  styles, 156–159
  ubiquitous nature of, 154
Cures Act, 99–101, 176
Cut-over strategy, 145

D

Dashboard thresholds, 23
Data, 133–137
  leading with, 37, 120
Data-informed decision-making, 124
Data migration, 208
Decision body meetings, 42, 91, 94, 123, 134
Decision-makers, 109
Decision-making bodies, 61, 84, 85, 90–94
  advisory members, 91
  chairperson, 91
  change requestor, 92–93
  clinical informaticist, 92
  facilitator, 92
  meeting recorder, 92
  observer members, 91–92
  organizer, 92
  voting members, 91
Decision rights, 123–124, 126, 212
Defect management software, 49, 59, 62, 65, 92
Defect management system, 139, 140, 148, 211

Defense Advance Research Project
        (DARPA), 54
Define, Measure, Analyze, Improve, and
        Control (DMAIC) improvement
        cycle, 45
Define work, 34, 38–40
Describe-and-defend model, 106
Design standards, 94–100
Design thinking, 3, 188–192, 195
    application, 192
    stages, 189, 190
Design work, 34–37
Diagnosis-related allegations, 203
Diagnosis-related group (DRG), 37
Discover work, 35, 37–38
Documentation, 130–132

E

Early wins, 133, 135, 137
eClinicalWorks, 5
EHR 1.0, 4, 7, 16, 20, 212
EHR 2.0 paradigm, 6–7, 16, 20, 212
EHR 3.0 paradigm, 7, 16, 62, 212–213
EHR-as-the-enemy, 20, 73, 74
EHR complexity, 73
EHR Governance Toolkit, xii, 17, 32, 49, 65,
        79, 102, 114, 196, 215
Eisenhower Box, 53–56
Electric vehicle (EV) market, 112
Electronic clinical quality measures
        (eCQMs), 35
Emergency department (ED), 14, 74
Emotional intelligence, 161
    identifying source of discomfort, 161
    looking on bright side, 163
    owning our part in situation, 162–163
    questioning basis of emotional response,
        161–162
Emotional piece, 160
Enjoyment culture values, 158
Entrepreneurship, 185–188
Envisioned future, 82
Epidemic Intelligence Service (EIS), 53
Equitability, 83
Establishing governance processes, 19–21
Ethics, principles of, 205–206

Evidence-based Knowledge Governance
        (EKG), 197–203
    decision body sign-off, 202
    document review, 199–200
    first-level review, 200–201
    lessons learned, 202–203
    opening change request, 201–202
Evidence-based medicine (EBM), 7, 38, 198
Evidence-based practice, 39
Expertise, 109
Expertise trap, 57
External clinical evidence, 38

F

Fairness, 83
The Family Medicine physician, 211
Fast Healthcare Interoperability Resources
        (FHIR®), 99–101, 188, 192
Firefighters, 177
First-In-First-Out (FIFO) principle, 86
Five As, 40
Food and Drug Administration (FDA), 5
Forward thinking, 29
Foundational interoperability, 98
Fractional numbers, 96
Funding, 70

G

Gamification, 180
Gantt chart, 25
Gartner hype cycle, 131–132
Gatekeeper function, 6, 61, 85–87, 101, 133,
        145, 199, 203–204, 212; *see also*
        routing
Gemba, 55, 120
Google Glass™ technology, 131
Governance bypass list, 32, 88
Governance dependencies, 33–37
    define work, 34, 38–40
    design work, 34–37
    discover work, 35, 37–38
Governance framework, 84–90
Governance Toolkit for EHR, xii, 17, 32, 49,
        65, 79, 102, 114, 196, 215
Group, 71

Guiding coalition, 67–79, 84, 117, 126, 163, 215

H

Healthcare organizations, 120, 158
Health Information Exchange (HIE), 99, 101, 132, 171
Health Information Technology (HIT), 7, 171
Health Information Management (HIM), 85, 128, 208
Health Information Technology for Economic and Clinical Health (HITECH) Act, 4, 5, 19, 172, 203
Health IT safely, 204
HIMSS Electronic Health Record Association (EHRA), 95
HL7® FHIR® Release, 4, 99, 100
Huddle, 67, 107, 114

I

Improve step, 45
Index Medicus, 40
Inertia, 55, 115–117, 125, 185
Informaticians, 6
Information Technology Infrastructure Library (ITIL), 169
Innovation, 185
Innovation areas, EHR onboarding, 179–180
Innovative leadership style, 29
  vs. command and control leader, 30
Instance alignment, 206–209
  key lessons, 206–209
Institute for Safe Medical Practices (ISMP), 95
Integrating the Healthcare Enterprise 4 (IHE), 100
Interoperability, 7, 8, 12–13, 36, 94, 98–100, 174–176, 192–193, 195
Interoperability rule, 176
Interstate Highway System, 54
Intrapreneurship, 185–188

J

Just culture, 68

K

Key results, 135–136
Key stakeholders, 20
KLAS analytics, 120, 130
KLAS Arch Collaborative, 19, 172–174, 182–183
  efficient governance structure, 176
  engaging training, 175
  personalization use, 176
  proactive interoperability, 175–176
  service-oriented support, 174–175
Kotter, John, 45–47, 53, 55

L

Land and expand, 156, 206
Law of inertia, 115
Law of instrument, 57
Leadership, 28, 67
Leading change model, 45
  anchoring changes, corporate culture, 47
  building on change, 47
  communicating vision, 46
  creating short-term wins, 47
  creating urgency, 45–46
  creating vision for change, 46
  forming powerful coalition, 46
  removing obstacles, 46–47
Leading with the data, 37, 120
Lean Six Sigma DMAIC methodology, 53
Learning culture values, 157
Learning curve, 75
Learning healthcare system, 34–35, 213–214
Legal, 203

M

MailChimp distribution list, 103
Maintenance, 88
Malpractice claims, 203–204
Mammography screening, 10, 11
Mastery, 7, 16, 70–71, 78, 116, 176
Mature governance framework, 197
Meaningful use, 5, 12, 16, 130
Measure step, 45
Medical Executive Committee (MEC) meetings, 43

Minimum viable product (MVP), 5, 90, 102
Mobile app, 133
Monitoring health IT, 204
Moral injury, 12–13
Multi-phasic order set, 187

N

Naïve realism, 76
National Academy of Medicine (NAM), 12
    clinician well-being and resilience, 13
National Comprehensive Cancer Network
    (NCCN), 209, 210
National Library of Medicine (NLM), 4
Natural language processing (NLP), 8
Nephrology decision-body group, 147
Net EHR Experience Score (NEES), 173,
    176–177
Newton's first law of motion, *see* Law of
    inertia
Nuance/M*Modal, 131
Nursing-initiated orders, 198

O

Objectives, 135, 136
Objectives and key results (OKRs),
    135–137
Office of the National Coordinator (ONC), 4,
    5, 192, 204
Onboarding new physicians, 179–181
Oncology physicians, 211
Oncology regimen governance, 149
Oncology regimen TAT, 211
Opportunity-driven urgency, 55
Opt-in tickets, 94
Order culture values, 158
Order set contents, 208
Order set review, *see* Evidence-based
        Knowledge Governance (EKG)
Oregon Health Sciences University
        (OHSU), 4
Organizational interoperability, 99
Organizational transformation, 169
Organizations adopting Lean, 44
OrthoVirginia (OV), 177–178
Overcentralizing decision-making, 124

Overcommunication, 104
Overpromising, 21

P

Parliamentary procedure, 93
Partnership, 72
Pathways to Proficiency program, 175
People, process, and technology framework,
    169 172
People-related factors, 176
Persuasion, 76–78
Pharmacy, partnering with, 144–146
Phone app, 104
Physician architect programs, 191
Physician builder, 191
Physician decision-making bodies, 84–85
Physician governance groups, 197
Physician leadership, 67
Physician–patient engagement, 73
Plan-do-study-act (PDSA) process, 44
Power, 69
Preventive Medicine and Public Health, 53
Principle of authority, 77
Principle of liking, 77
Principle of reciprocity, 77
Principle of social proof, 77
Printer mappings, 207
Prioritization scoring tool, 26
Process-related factors, 176
Proof-of-concept, 53, 202, 209
Provider Support Specialist (PSS), 177, 178
Proxy, 93
Purpose, 7, 16, 55, 68, 70–71, 78, 82–83, 101
    culture values, 157
Pyramid of Change, 23, 24, 178

Q

Quality improvement (QI), 35
    tools, 73
Quantitative baseline metrics, 128
Quorum, 6, 93, 146–147, 149, 151

R

Recovery Audit Contract (RAC), 130
Reflective listening, 76

Research-based evidence, 39
Resisters, 120–122
Resourcing, 86
Results culture values, 158
Right channel, 11
Right format, 11
Right information, 10
Right person, 10
Right time in workflow, 11–12
Routing, 85–87, 101, 145, 199, 203, 212
Routing committee, 85, 87
Rule of thumb, 89, 186

S

Sackett's hierarchy of evidence pyramid, 39
Safe health IT, 204
SAFER guides, 204, 215
Safety culture values, 158
Savvy providers, 130
SBARs, 94, 108, 113
Scaling process, 140–146
Scarcity, 77
Scoring tools, 26–27, 32
    complexity, 27
    prioritization, 26
Scribes, 131
Self-serve dashboard, 133
Semantic interoperability, 99
Sequencing, 111
Service level agreements (SLAs), 22, 118
Setting expectations and priorities, 21–27
Shorter-term targets, 47
Similarity, 111
Simplify™, 191
Situation, Background, Assessment,
    Recommendation (SBAR) format,
    94, 108, 113
Six Sigma DMAIC cycle of process
    improvement, 45
Social science literature, 156
Software needs, 41–43
    collaboration tool, 42
    data analysis, 43
    defect tracking, 41
    document repository, 41
    meeting software, 41–42

visualization tools, 43
Solution jumping, 56–58, 64–65
Specialty-specific user interfaces, 128–130
Status quo bias, 115
    break free tips, 117
Stop-gap solution, 193
Stories, 133
Strategy, 16, 19, 28, 54–55, 81–102, 104, 129,
    145, 153–155, 159, 161–162, 165, 177,
    207, 212
Structural interoperability, 99
Subject matter experts (SMEs), 91
Success, 160

T

Teams, 67–71
Telehealth services, 171, 192–195
Thinking piece, 160
Three Ds (define, design, and discover)
    model, 33–37, 171, 213
Three-legged stool/golden triangle, 170
Throughput, 23, 31, 63, 86, 118,
    126, 133
Time-honored approach, 111
Top-down requests, 28
Training, 27, 86–87, 121, 128, 131, 135, 160,
    173–176, 179–183, 207
Transparency core value, 83
Trusted communicator, 109
Trustworthiness, 110
Turn-around time (TAT), 22–23, 31, 118,
    126, 133, 146, 210–211

U

Unfreeze-change-refreeze model, 45
Unified care delivery model, 212
United States Core Data for Interoperability
    (USCDI), 99, 192
United States Preventive Services Task
    Force, 10
UPS tracking system, 133
UpToDate®, 8
Urgency needed for change, 55–56
Usability principle, 54
User-centric, 84, 90, 101, 105, 188

User experience, 128, 135, 141, 146, 153, 169–183, 188
  survey, 119
uTrace™ app, 22, 190–191

V

Value stream mapping, 44
Vendors, 5
Virtual asynchronous communication platform, 146
Virtual communication platform, 211
Virtual governance process, 146–150
Virtual teams, matrixed organizations, 107
Visio diagrams, 108, 109

Vision, 81
Voice and choice, 15, 67, 83, 212
Voice of customer, 27–31
Voice-only meetings, 42
Voice-to-text software, 131
Voice-to-text technology tools, 131

W

Well-meaning administrators, 28
Well-respected voices, 156
Wong-Baker FACES pain rating scale, 36
Word cloud, 119
Workflow-driven documentation, 131

Milton Keynes UK
Ingram Content Group UK Ltd.
UKHW050450071024
449327UK00014B/317